MUSLIM SOCIETY IN TRANSITION

(A STUDY OF HYDERABAD)

MUSLIM SOCIETY IN TRANSITION

(A STUDY OF HYDERABAD)

ARIFA KULSOOM JAVED

COMMONWEALTH PUBLISHERS
NEW DELHI INDIA

The Publication has been Financially Supported by the Indian Council of Social Sciences Research, NEW DELHI, and the Responsibility of the Facts Stated, opinions expressed and Conclusions Reached is entirely that of the author and I.C.S.S.R. accepts no Responsibility for them.

I.C.S.S.R. consultant
Prof. IMTIAZ AHMED

First Published, 1992

ISBN 81-7169-096-3

Published by:
AJAY VERMA
COMMONWEALTH PUBLISHERS
4378/4-B, MURARI LAL STREET
ANSARI ROAD, DARIYAGANJ
NEW DELHI-110002 (INDIA)
3272541

Printed at:
EFFICIENT OFFSET PRINTERS
215, SHAHZADA BAGH, PHASE-II
DELHI - 110035

This book is dedicated
to the profound memory of my
ever-inspiring research guide
Dr. A.R. Saiyed.

FOREWORD

Academic research on the social and cultural life of Muslim communities in India has been characterized by three principal deficiencies. First, it has been focused far too much on the traditional social organization of Muslim communities and has remained caught up into the question whether or not the social groups one encounters in traditional Muslim social organization are comparable to caste. Second, and perhaps because of preoccupation with whether or not the traditional Muslim social groups are castes, it has overlooked analysis of Muslim social class structure and the changes which have taken place in it from time to time in response to social and economic developments events of far-reaching social significance. Finally, it has very substantially ignored the study the socio-psychological impact of cataclysmic events such as partition which brought about an upheaval in Muslim society in this country or other social developments such as the oil boom in the Gulf countries and the consequent external migration from which very large numbers of Muslims in several parts of India were able to benefit. The research reported in the following pages is refreshing in that it focuses very greatly on these relatively neglected areas of Muslim social and cultural life in India.

The author's concern in this work is an exploration of social change among the muslims of Hyderabad. Her analysis of social change is not cast within the typical format of what is commonly described as a then and now study. Instead, it analysis social change sequentially through three time dimensions separated by the social upheaval generated by Police Action and the removal of the Nizam of Hyderabad from his pre-eminent position as the ruler of Hyderabad State, it begins by constructing a picture of traditional Muslim social and cultural life-particularly Muslim social class structure-as it had evolved over the centuries and existed at the time of Police Action in 1947. Then it analyses the social and psychological trauma that police Action caused and the kinds of social and psychological problems which it created for members of the different social classes of Hyderabadi Muslim society. Finally, the study examines the process of adjustment to the traumatic changes precipitated by Police Action and what kind of social organization has been taking shape over the period following the social upheaval caused by Police Action.

Anyone familiar with Hyderabad knows too well that police Action was a cataclysmic event in the life of Hyderabadi Muslims, perhaps comparable in its magnitude and impact upon the life of Hyderabadi Muslims to that of partition on the life of Muslims in north India. It not only resulted in the abolition of the erstwhile Muslim princely State of Hyderabad, which was its obvious consequence, but initiated a process of social reorganization as the very first around which the fabric of Hyderabadi Muslim social life had become woven was suddenly removed. From then on, the traditional Muslim aristocracy which had successfully sustained the traditional Muslim Social class structure as well the highly elaborate cultural life styles which served as the basis of distinguishing one social class from another suffered a decline, forming way for processess of social mobility previously unknown. The oil boom and the flow of petrodollars to sections of Hyderabadi Muslims who, having been displaced by the decline in their socio-economic situation as a result of the growing inability of the Muslim aristocracy to sustain the traditional social class structure, has been an additional factor in prompting social mobility. This book seeks to delineate these social currents and cross-currents in considerable detail, focusing specifically on Muslim social class structure, positional changes of families within particular social classes and the changing position of women in Hyderabadi Muslim society.

Encompassing three time dimensions covering a period of over half a century would require studying society at different time periods as well as at different levels. This could be done either by recourse to historical records or by talking to individuals who have passed through the viccitudes of times and events and are in-a position to offer and integrated account of what they saw and lived through. The reconstruction of the picture of Hyderabadi Muslim society and social organization which the author has attempted in this work is not based on an exploration of historical materials through insights drawn from that material are often used to probe into empirical realities. It is based instead upon oral biographies and detailed and intensive interviews the author collected from reliable informants. Further, the author has not confined this study to a delineation of the macro picture of social change that emerges from the oral biographies and the detailed and intensive interview data. The author goes on to compare and match this macro picture through a more circumscribed sociological study at the micro level. On the whole, through the methodology of intensive and holistic field work the author has been able not only to delineate the social changes but also to ascertain and verify that her account of changes at the macro level indeed fits in with the picture which emerges from an exploration of the sociological realities at the micro level.

Monographic works on Muslim communities in India have been seriously lacking. It is, indeed, commendable that through publication of her research the author has taken a step towards bridging this yawning gap in the sociological study of Muslims in India. Equally, it is heartening that this work deals with the social life of Hyderabadi Muslims about whom little sociological research has so far been available. One is assured in the pages which follow of an absorbing treatment of a people and a theme both of whom have not been previously subjected to serious sociological investigation.

Imtiaz Ahmed

New Delhi
April, 1992

PREFACE

Partition of India was a traumatic experience when the people of the sub-continent were divided into two nations with their own destinies. The incident in-fact opened fresh avenues of study in various branches of sociology, particularly in the field of community studies and social change.

This book is an attempt to study the impact of this political change on the Muslim community of Hyderabad who continued to be the ruling elite not only till the partition of the country but even thirteen months later, till the amalgamation of the state of Hyderabad with the Indian Union. Muslims of Hyderabad experienced a sudden loss of power and dominance when the inevitable occured. The Muslim state which was eventually carved in the south by different dynasties of Bahmanis, Qutubhahis and Asaf Jahis was brought in the mainstream of united India. A distinct culture was taken away its boundaries. A peculiar social order which was nurtured by the benevalent kings of three different dynasties lost its peculiarities under the new changes. A state which proved to be an island of peace and security during the freedom struggle of 1857 for all the Indians was now at the mercy of the decisions at Delhi.

Immediately after police Action there was a challenge of survival for the Muslims due to the disintegration of the feudal order. Abolition of the Jagirs and retrenchment of Muslims from the services turned them into paupers. A few actively involved in the Razakar movement migrated to Pakistan, but it did not solve the problem of the majority of Muslims. They stayed back in Hyderabad alongwith the Nizam who also opted for the same even after the loss of power.

Present research is an attempts to study the period following police action marked by a vacaum of sociological literature bringing out the disintegration and plight of police action. It is perhaps one of the first studies with two important features. Firstly, it takes into account the differential impact of change on all the three different stratas of the Muslim society i.e. upper, middle and lower. Another important feature of this study is that it covers a very vast canvas, beginning with the pre-police action grandeur, the plight of police action, the gloom and disintigration that followed police action and finally the changes in contemporary Muslim society due to oil boom of the Gulf and the remittances pouring into Hyderabad city.

Since it is a pioneering work of its kind and there is an absolute dearth of sociological literature the author was posed with a methodological challenge for the collection of primary and secondary data, both. She had to rely on the information provided by the informants and respondents along with her own participant observation.

It may be admitted that a study like this has not been able to either depend upon or generate a theoretical formulation regarding the sociological understanding of social change. To a certain extent Arnold Toynbee's theory of challenge and response was found relevant in the present context. The situation that was surveyed and studied was culturally as well as historically specific. Such situations and their studies do not easily lend themselves to any theorizing. Though it has been successful in bringing out certain important trends of change among Hyderabadi Muslims the nature of the study continued to be exploratory descriptive rather than analytical. But it follow up studies are undertaken some theoretical analysis can hopefully emerge.

ARIFA K. JAVED

CONTENTS

1

Introduction and Methodology

Introduction

Muslims in India constitute about 12% of the total population of the country. This figure is larger than that to be found in the different Muslim countries excepting Bangladesh or Indonesia. Indian Muslims like their Hindu brethren, and in keeping with the regional diversities that characterise Indian, do not constitute a monolithic entity. Notwithstanding a common religion, they are differentiated with well marked cultural differences which are primarily regional in character. Some of these regional characteristics have been accentuated due to historical reasons. Thus, for example, in north India the Kingdom of Avadh with its epicentre in Lucknow, promoted a typical Muslim dominated culture which had a spirit and flavour not to be found among Muslim subcultures elsewhere in the country. Similar to the development of the "Lucknawi culture", the city of Hyderabad also saw the efflorescence of a very unique culture and society which came to be typified as "Deccani", which may also be described as "Hyderabadi".

Unlike in north India, where they became a dominant group because of invasions and conquests, in south India, Muslims generally entered and settled as migrants and traders. However among the few exceptions to this general situation was their dominance over Hyderabad. Here Muslims entered as rulers.

Inevitably, on account of their elitist position, they

developed a distinct socio-cultural ethos. However, this distinct ethos was very different from the Indo-Muslim culture that had developed in north India as a result of more than six centuries of Muslim rule. The Deccani or Hyderabadi Muslim culture was a synthesis of the royal culture of Iran (which the Qutub Shahis had brought with them) and the Mughal culture (brought by the Mughal Subedar) and the local Hindu culture of Dravidian origin ; Hindus and Muslims were equal co-sharers in it. This synthetic culture flowered considerably because of the relative harmony that existed between Muslims and Hindus in the socio-cultural and economic spheres, notwithstanding the fact that the Muslim rulers had caused a political replacement of Hindu rule. Possibly, the Muslim rulers' acceptance of, and encouragement to, the local culture had a great deal to do with the development of this synthetic culture.

The fact that the Hindu subjects were generally not victimized, and were not subjected to the discriminatory *Jazia* (a special tax on non-Muslims only) but were, instead, recruited into the Muslim army, as well as in the administrative machinery during the rule of both the Qutub Shahis and Asaf Jahis (during which periods state grants were freely receiveb by Hindu temples), contributed to the emergence, stabilization and acceptance of this syncretic culture. Eventually, large numbers of Hindus adopted this synthesis and remained under its sway throughout the period of Muslim ascendancy in Hyderabad, which was spread over a period of almost five centuries, that is, 1518 to 1948.

The foundation of the composite Hyderabadi way of life began to be shaken when the Indian subcontinent became a victim of the communal passions and violence which eventually culminated in the partition of the country. Hyderabad, as a centre of Muslim dominance and Muslim elitism, obviously could not survive in the historical form it had assumed under its two Muslim dynasties. In September, 1948, the inevitable occurred and the flag of Asaf Jahi ruler Mir Osman Ali Khan, known to the world as the fabulously wealthy Nizam, (or the richest man on earth) was replaced by the Indian tricolour. The wheel of history had turned round and Muslim dominance, which five centuries ago had replaced Hindu rule, had to make way for the re-establishment of a Hindu-based policy, though, of course, within the secular framework of the Indian Constitution.

While the partition of the country was, in many respects, a disaster for the Muslims of divided India, the tragedy of Hyderabadi Muslims in several respects was a more serious one. Unlike north Indian Muslims who had lost power to the British more than a century ago, Hyderabadi Muslims continued to be the ruling elite even after India was partitioned in 1947. But following the dissolution of the Asaf Jahi dynasty in 1948, they overnight suffered a role reversal and lost their pre-eminent position in the state. Power and dominance, and along with these the society and culture that had been built over a period of five centuries rapidly vanished/disintegrated and for Hyderabadi Muslims, whether they belonged to the elite class or the masses, glory evaporated into nothingness.

Loss of political and economic supremacy led to fundamental changes in Hyderabadi Muslim society. Following the Police Action, and the unsavoury incidents, thereafter, Muslims took to migration, first to Pakistan and then to the West. Muslim learning, and other contributions to literature, art and culture dried off and suddenly a dynamic and vibrant culture came to a standstill. The economic decline of Muslim feudals, and the relative absence of the professional middle class, altered the social structure and simultaneously gave rise to various socio-cultural, socio-economic and socio-political problems.

But the pessimism that had seized the Muslim mind soon after Police Action, and which had led Hyderabadi Muslims to believe that there was no future for them, fortunately, was not to last long. Their trials and tribulations considerably receded into the background as the larger Indian society embarked upon the path of modernization and development. This process, and certain international developments, helped Hyderabadi Muslims to pull themselves out of the gloom that had enveloped them after 1948. Having once been a dynamic community, it gradually began to take advantage of the new opportunities availabe to them.

In the seventies, the global phenomenon of petrodollar affluence particularly came as a boon for Hyderabadi Muslims. To large segments of this community, petrodollars brought a wealth that has helped them to recreate, to a considerable extent, a past which they had once thought was entirely lost and gone. Though no measure of re-creation of the past could fully restore what once was and the present was nothing but an amalgam of various trends and strains with some influences of the past.

Thus, as one surveys the Hyderabadi Muslim scene, one sees a vast panorama of several interesting changes that have occurred in the life of this community over a period of about forty years or so. For the sociologists these changes are of immense interest and significance. They need to be systematically studied both in order to understand how the forces of modernism and tradition intermingle in the life of a distinct community ; as well as, at a more macro level, to understand the dynamics of the process of social change which has fascinated sociologists since the very time its founding fathers turned their attention to this interesting discipline.

Surprisingly, there appear to be no studies dealing with the changes of traumatic period following Police Action. Possibly the community had been left too benumbed even to register its reactions in academic forms. Thus the entire period of the 1950s and 1960s went unnoticed. Since, there exist virtually no accounts written by social scientists of this period, the present study has tried to fill up this gap by resorting to data collection on the basis of "oral" history. The researcher contacted a large number of senior Muslim residents of Hyderabad who had experienced those traumatic days, in order to build up an account of what happened to the traditional feudal order and how the Muslim society responded, when confronted by the forces of disintegration.

The second major event was the opening up of employment opportunities in the Gulf countries. For reasons, explained later in the thesis, Hyderabadi Muslims were favourably positioned to take advantage of these opportunities. The study attempts to examine the impact of petrodollars upon the Muslims of the city, many of whom had become victims of deep frustration in the three decades following the aftermath of Police Action.

Accordingly, the specific objectives of the study are as under :

1. To develop an ethnographic account of the traditional culture and society of Hyderabadi Muslims.
2. To describe the socio-economic and socio-cultural impact of partition, and Police Action, upon Hyderabadi Muslims.
3. To analyse the kind and extent of change and modernization that is being reflected in social life, and to evaluate the role of remittance economy in this change.
4. (Considering that change affects different social strata, differentially), to examine how different social strata of Hyderabadi Muslims have responded to change.

Of course, it was not feasible in one single enquiry to make a study of all aspects of Hyderabadi Muslim society. Hence, to keep the study within manageable limits, the researcher endeavoured to focus particular attention upon :

(a) Migrations, the changing occupational structure and intergenerational mobility in last four decades.

(b) The impact of petrodollars upon the social life of Hyderabadi Muslims with special emphasis on changing life styles, status of woman, education and employment.

In attempting the task in hand as indicated above the study developed a macro view of social change in Hyderabadi Muslim society. In doing so, an effort was made to capture (and revived for its information) old memories, which, however, needed some empirical support. To fulfil this shortcoming, a survey of 160 families was also made and data was collected on some of the dimensions that had emerged in the macro view of change. The findings of this survey have been presented as "micro analysis" in the last part of the book.

Finally it may be mentioned that the author herself hails from Hyderabad, and has personally witnessed and experienced several of the events described here. Of course many of these did not appear in the same light as they eventually did when she returned to her home town fortified with the perceptions and skills of a research student in Sociology. Nevertheless, she enjoyed the advantage of being an "Insider". This also helped her to overcome some of the problems which some other researcher not similarly positioned might have encountered. All in all, the work on this study has been a "labour of love" for her.

As stated earlier, the present research is an attempt to study social change in the Muslim society of Hyderabad, with reference to the period following the Police Action of 1948, as a consequence of which the five and a half century long Muslim rule came to an end in Hyderabad state, the feudal order dissolved, and the socio-economic and socio-political fortunes of Hyderabadi Muslims underwent a sea change. Besides 1948, the early 1970s (when the oil boom of the Gulf countries began), represent another landmark for Hyderabadi Muslims inasmuch as the oil boom had a more profound impact upon these Muslims than perhaps anyother single subcultural Muslim group in this country. Thus the study of social change of the Muslim society of Hyderabad from 1948 till 1985 can be conveniently divided into two phases: first from 1948 to 1970 and second from 1970s onwards. The timeframe of the present study is therefore spread over an approximate period of four decades.

Since the study of change and modernization of any group, community or society must take into cognisance the traditional character or period of that society, it was necessary in the present study to first reconstruct an account of the traditional feudal social order that had existed prior to 1948.

Accordingly the present study is divided into three parts. The first part focuses attention upon the traditional social structure and culture of the Muslims of Hyderabad; the second part is concerned with an analysis of the factors responsible for, and the character of changes, following the Police Action, and, finally, the third part is devoted to the period following the oil boom.

Micro and Macro Perspective

The present study involved a methodological challenge. Since it covered a time span of four decades and more, in which certain very profound and far-reaching exogenous factors had affected Hyderabadi Muslims. A micro analysis based on the study of a small group would not have done adequate justice to the importance of the topic. On the other hand, to go back in the time and reconstruct change on the basis of extremely limited secondary data and interviews with knowledgeable informants would have yielded a macro view but without suitable empirical support. This would have indicated some very broad contours of change, such a view would have lacked the confidence that comes from empirical support at the micro level. Therefore a research strategy was developed which allowed for the study of change both at the macro and micro level.

Universe and the Setting

The universe broadly speaking was the city of Hyderabad and covered groups and individuals belonging to various socio-economic strata. Specifically the study was conducted with the help of informants and respondents primarily in the following localities and *mohallas*: Aliabad, Jahanuma, Dana-ki-Bawli, Mittikasher, Hussaini Alum, Panchi Burraq, Musa Bawli, Chaurasta, Kurmaguda, Chanchalguda, Yakutpura, Azampura, Chadarghat, Kachiguda, Turoop Bazar, Hyderguda, Himayat Nagar, Bashir Bagh, Adarsh Nagar, Nampalli, Agapura, Lakdi-ka-Pul, Masab Tank, Mehdipatnam, Humayun Nagar, Banjara Hills, Jubilee Hills, Somajiguda and Panjagutta.

The interviews were conducted on the basis of an interview guide specifically prepared for the purpose. Due to an unstructured format there was a free flow of information. Each informant was encouraged to reconstruct the past on the basis of memories and experiences. This "oral history" approach has been a special feature of the methodology of the present study.

This tool of "oral history" was exclusively utilized to collect data concerning events immediately following Police Action as secondary data for this period was virtually non-existent.

The opportunity provided to the informants to enter into the realm of "oral history" turned out to be a very rewarding experience, inasmuch as for many of them it was the first systematic effort to seek data from them concerning the events of a period which they had seen and experienced, which they remembered with nostalgia, and, about which they wanted to talk but had found few patient research-oriented listeners.

It is obvious that informants in such a process originally begin with a nucleus of some four or five individuals, but eventually multiply due to the snow-ball effect. The most suitable occasions for meeting the well-educated representatives of Hyderabadi Muslims were various seminars of Osmania University and functions in the well-known Jubilee Hall, in the city. The researcher would seize the opportunities to briefly introduce herself and the topic of research, and she was willingly given appointments at their residence.

In the course of interviewing these informants, the researcher had to be careful enough to both keep up the interests of informants so that they enjoyed recalling pains and pleasures of the past, as well as to continuously keep the interview within well-defined boundaries so that she could obtain data along lines that were relevant and useful for her. Due to the differing socio-economic backgrounds and experiences of the informants, the resultant data was rich and varied in nature and helped the researcher to obtain a balanced and well-rounded perspective. Thus informants who had been civil servants at the time of Police Action were more interested in narrating facts about the Action and its aftermath, since they were in service at that time and had been eye-witnesses to the various events of those critical days. Such informants gave their accounts in rather broad and general terms, while those from the lower social strata made their accounts more personal. Similarly, informants who at that time were in the various administrative units of the Nizam's Government, and were compulsorily given premature retirement, particularly provided information about the pre-Police Action traditional social order as it had existed under the last Nizam.

Obviously, the varied background of the informants demanded a great amount of skill on the part of the researcher in directing these interviews in a manner that could elicit data relevant for her purpose.

Informants and Respondents

(1) *Informants*: These were the old educated and knowledgeable Hyderabadi citizens above the age of 55 years who had experienced feudal life under the Nizam, and in 1948 had passed through the trauma of Police Action, and were in a position to give first hand information, with relevant insights about the topic of research from their personal experiences. Since they had experienced four decades or more of profound changes in their lives, they served an excellent source of "oral history" concerning the changes that have occurred in Hyderabadi Muslim society.

The initial nucleus of informants was constituted by the researcher's own relatives, family friends and the domestic servants and beggars who were associated with her family for generations. Eventually, the number of the informants went on expanding as a chain got linked up in which one informant helped her to contact others, and so on.

(2) *Respondents*: For the micro analysis a sample of 160 respondents of three different social strata was selected with 50 respondents each from the upper and middle classes and 60 from the lower class. This sample size was found to be adequate because the method of data collection from these respondents involved the collection of family histories, on the basis of a suitable interview scheduled covering three successive generations of each respondent.

In contrast to the informants who were interviewed for reconstructing a macro perspective and obtaining qualitative data, the respondents were approached for obtaining quantitative data with a view to construct a micro perspective.

This technique of data collection through family histories was found to be very useful and rewarding as it captured data on social change over a pariod of time. The data regarding three successive generations in the same family provided empirical evidence pertaining to intergenerational mobility, change in occupational structure, migrations and overseas employment, all of which were the concerns of the present study.

Like the informants, the respondents also belonged to the age group 55 years or more, who gave all the desired information about their parents themselves and their children. Almost all these 160 respondents were introduced by the informants who had repeatedly used these respondent families as examples in their "oral histories" to narrate various incidences of social change. Thus it was easy to cross-check the information provided by the respondents.

The upper class respondents included civil servants, doctors, engineers, judges and lawyers and university teachers. The middle class respondents included school teachers, health inspectors (para medical staff), supervisors (diploma holding engineers), clerks and typists. The lower class was further divided into skilled workers and unskilled wage earners. Skilled workers included drivers, tailor, welders and electricians, and unskilled wage earners included domestic servants, rickshaw-pullers and beggars.

The specific dimensions tapped in these family histories were :

(a) Occupational mobility in three successive generations.

(b) Change in educational attainments.

(c) Migration to western countries.

(d) Overseas employment.

(e) Change in quality of life due to repatriation.

Collectively, this dada is indicative of the type of changes which each generation in the three different strata underwent.

2

Rise and Fall of Muslim Supremacy in Hyderabad

Historical Background

Muslims in India acquired political dominance on the plateau of Deccan with the invasion by Allauddin Khilji in 1310 A.D. on the Kakatiya empire of Warangal. This marks the beginning of Muslim supremacy in Hyderabad region which continued till 17th September, 1948.

Mohammad-Bin-Tughlaq, who ascended the throne of Delhi in 1325 after Allauddin Khilji, shifted his capital from Delhi to Deogiri, renaming it Daulatabad. However Tughlaq did not stay there for a long time and shifted the capital back to Delhi leaving Deccan in the hands of local governors. In 1338, as the Delhi sultanate weakened, the governor Zafar Khan Allauddin Shah Bahman declared himself the ruler of Deccan including Gulburga and Bidar. This marks the beginning of an independent Muslim rule on the plateau of Deccan. It is known as the Bahmini dynasty.

As the Bahmini kingdom weakened, its various subedars declared themselves to be independent rulers. By 1527 the Bahmini kingdom disintegrated into four Muslim states under different dynasties. Of interest for present purpose is the Qutub Shahi dynasty. The foundation of this dynasty was laid in 1518 by Quli Qutub Shah who was the subedar of Telangana in the erstwhile Bahmini Kingdom. He declared himself an independent ruler, with Golconda as his capital.

The Qutub Shahi territory extended from Warangal to Machhlipatnam. This dynasty produced in all seven rulers of whom Ibrahim Quli Qutub Shah and Sultan Mohammad Quli Qutub Shah are important because their reigns saw the emergence of a new cultural entity which eventually came to be known as the "Deccani Culture".

The period of Ibrahim Quli Qutub Shah marks a golden period in the history of this dynasty. He was well-versed in Telugu, and had a personal liking for the culture of Telangana. His reign saw the beginning of cultural integration of Hindus and Muslims, which led to an era of communal harmony that was to last for centuries, Ibrahim Qutub Shah was popularly known among his Hindu subjects as "Ibrahimdu".

Sultan Mohammad Quli Qutub Shah succeeded Ibrahim Quli Qutub Shah and ascended the throne in 1580. He continued the task of cultural integration and further nurtured the composite culture of Telangana into a distinct cultural entity. His achievements also included the construction of beautiful buildings, palaces, including the famous Charminar and Darus-Shafa (the present Unani hospital). The choice of the site for Charminar, where the old city is situated now, was made because of the sentimental attachment of the king to this place. His beloved, Bhagmati lived in Chichlam, a village situated somewhere near the site of Charminar. To immortalize his attachment to that place the king built the famous monument of Charminar. The city of Hyderabad was planned around this monument. Beautiful gardens were implanted and canals were constructed around Charminar. Hyderabad city was initially called Bhagyanagar after Bhagyamati. Later, when she was given the title of Hyder Mahal, the city was renamed Hyderabad.

During this period, Golconda became the centre of trade and touched new height of prosperity. The fame of its diamonds, steel and printed cloth attracted people from both Asia and Europe.

Mohammad Quli Qutub Shah was also a good poet and patronized art, literature and the new cultural entity, the

Deccani culture, which had emerged during the period of his father.

After these two rulers the fortunes of this dynasty declined because the successor, Abdullah Quli Qutub Shah, was a minor and could not protect his territory against repeated attacks by the Mughals. He ruled under the guardianship of his mother, Hayat Bakshi Begum, and grand mother Khanam Agha. Unfortunately at this time, the Mughals started invading Deccan and Golconda facing the assault and battery. A treaty was signed with the Mughals according to which the kingdom of Golconda had to pay an annual tribute to the Mughal Empire.

Abdullah Qutub Shah was succeeded by his son-in-law, Tana Shah. Though under the subordinatation of Mughals, Tana Shah performed ably. He paid special attention to agriculture, strengthening irrigation sources by constructing dams and tanks. He also improved the procedures of revenue collection, rehabilitated ruined villages, restructured the department of mining and made improvements in the *aukaf*.

Notwihstanding all this, Golconda became a part of the Mughal empire in the year 1687, when Aurangzeb finally conquered Golconda. With this annexation, the centre for power shifted from Hyderabad to Aurangabad which became the headquarters of the Deccan province of the Mughal Empire.

On the whole, the Qutub Shahi dynasty made remarkable contributions to the social and cultural history of Hyderabad, and laid the foundation of cultural unity among the different communities of the state.

With the downfall of Mughal Empire, the centre at Delhi became weak and political instability percolated down to Deccan. This had a retarding effect on the life and society of the city of Hyderabad. But political conditions got restabilized by the end of 1725, when the subedar of Deccan Qamaruddin Khan Asaf Jah/declared himself the king of Hyderabad under the title Asaf Jah I and founded the Asaf Jahi dynasty. This was again a continuation of Muslim rule on the plateau of Deccan with Hyderabad as its capital. Thereafter Hyderabad remained under the Asaf Jahi flag for about two and a quarter centuries, from 1725-1948. For some time Hyderabad became a victim of Anglo-French rivalry but eventually the British succeeded and brought Nizam Ali Khan to the throne in 1761, with the title of Asaf Jah II. The British developed close political connections with the Asaf Jahi rulers and when India came under the British crown after 1857, a Resident was appointed in the Nizam's State.

In his historical account *Tareekh-e-Daccan*, Abdul Ghafoor Khan (1903) writes that thc westerners not only established trade relations but were also employed as incharge of cannonry, horticulture, and as state physicians. They had tremendous adaptability in them. They easily adopted the Muslim culture as it was the culture of the ruling class. However, these foreigners were an object of mockery. Their dress and life style was held in low esteem. Local people considered it a sin to emulate their manners and western education was intensely hated. But this hatred did not last for very long. Within a very short time members of the elite started employing English and Anglo-Indian governesses for their children and sending them to English medium schools. Thus, by the turn of the century, the Muslim elite had come under the impact of western education and westernization. This cultural change put it in good stead in the days following the Police Action of 1948, when several members of the elite families fled to U.K. and U.S.A. to escape from the humiliations of a changed fortune.

Since we are here concerned with the phenomenon of social change that was initiated during the period of Nizam VII Mir Osman Ali Khan, it is proposed, in what follows, to describe in detail the social, cultural, economic and political conditions of his times. This has been attempted in the following chapters. Immediately, however, attention has been devoted in the present chapter to the efforts of the last descendent of the Asaf Jahi dynasty to modernize Hyderabad, and the political events on the subcontinent which overwhelmed him, and led to the extinguishment of this dynasty.

Modernization of Hyderabad State under the Last Nizam

Nawab Mir Osman Ali Khan the VIIth Nizam, ascended the throne in the year 1911. He was a man of modern outlook, much ahead of his times. By this far-sightedness and originality of ideas he tried to develop Hyderabad state on modern lines. Unlike his predecessors, he devoted much of his time to the affairs of the state, keeping himself aloof from the luxuries of feudal life. He tried to wean away the nobles from their easy going and extravagant ways of life, and made them useful members of the society by appointing them to responsible positions and keeping a constant watch on their performance. He tried to break the mental stagnation and indifference of his subjects by spreading education, and increasing employment opportunities through the public works programme.

A brief account of his contribution to the development of Hyderabad will provide a proper background to the main theme of the study. We begin, however, with a brief account of the socio-economic organization and politico-administrative set-up of feudal Hyderabad.

State owned land, which was the main source of income, was divided into three major categories: Crown land (*Sarfekhas*), State land (*Diwani*) and the land of the nobles (*Jagirs*), of all sizes and ranks.

Diwani land was 58% of the total of the state. The remaining 42% was divided into *Sarfekhas* and *Jagirs*. The revenue of *Sarfekhas* land was administered by a separate administration and the income from this source was the personal income of the king, and was utilized for the personal expenditure of the king and his family (Mudiraj, 1934).

This institution was a major source of employment for the Muslims. No specific qualifications were prescribed to hold any post in the administration. Relationship with the royal or noble families was the chief consideration for the higher posts. For the lower posts, relationship with high officials was the main consideration for securing a job, provided the job seeker could read and write Urdu and knew elementary arithmetic. Those who were employed learnt the requirements of their jobs through experience (Hassan, 1967).

There was a practice to give a temporary appointment in the beginning for a sufficiently long period, and then grant permanancy. Many Muslim families received their livelihood from this arrangement. It is reported that they happily accepted these jobs and lived a contented life, even though salaries were meagre. Lacking in educational qualifications, these people were not in a position to get better jobs. Promotional avenues were rare and retirement age was not fixed. Many of the old respondents (interviewed for the study) expressed satisfaction that even the small monthly income of Rs. 20 of that time provided them more comfortable living than the present day income running into hundreds of rupees.

Diwani land was organized by the Revenue Department of the Government. There was a streamlined system of collecting land revenue and excise duties from the rural population. The state was divided into provinces (*Suba*), Districts, *Taluqas* and villages, for this purpose. There were Commissioners (*Subedars*), Collectors and Deputy Collectors (*Talqdars* and *Du'am Talqdars*) and revenue inspectors (*Tahsildars*). Muslims were in overwhelming majority on all these posts. Again, appointments were given to the members of the royal and noble families, on these posts. At lower level there was an important post of *Patwari*, who was the main record-keeper of land at the village level. These posts were in the possession of local Hindus. It was an inherited job.

Jagir land was under the supervision of *jagirdars*. Certain big *jagirs*, under the stewardship of the highest nobility, were actually states within the state. Originally, these *jagirs* were allotted by the king as a reward of loyalty and bravery. Members of the royal family were also allotted *jagirs* for their maintenance. *Jagir* rights were transferred from generation to generation. *Jagir* administration was independent in administrative, revenue and judicial matters. *Jagirdars* also maintained their own army. The reason for this was that *jagirdars* would supply armed forces to the king wherever it was needed. The *jagirdar* was the chief of the army, judiciary, police and civil adminstration in the same manner as the king in the state. Majority of those employed in all these activities were Muslims. Administration was generally slack and welfare activities were non-existent. People living in the area were at the whims of the *jagirdar*; a person could be rewarded for nothing, if the *jagirdar* was pleased, and punished severely also for nothing at all if the *jagirdar* was displeased.

Feudal lords were from amongst both the communities, Hindus and Muslims. By nature they were comfort loving and non-industrious. As a result, the entire development in industry and trade that had taken place had been effected by government, and a few enlightened individuals from both the communities. The Muslims who contributed to the urban-industrial growth were mostly from outside the state.

There existed in the Nizam's government a department known as "Court of Wards", which looked after the *jagir* affairs if the heirs were minors. In case of a general complaint of maladministration of the *jagir* affairs, the department took over the charge of the *jagir* and managed it temporarily. This action was known as *zabti*. The errant *jagirdar* was to beseech the Nizam and tender his apologies with assurance of good conduct. After a period of trial if the ruler was satisfied, orders for the release of land were passed. This action was known as *Bahali* or *Waguzasht*. This was mostly done in case of small *jagirs*. The "Courts of Wards" department was always full of such cases (Mudiraj, 1934).

Besides *jagirs*, lande was also allotted to places of religious importance like mosques., *dargahs* and temples; this land was known as *magta* (state donated land). The caretaker of this place was called *mutawali* or *magtedar*. *Magta* land was also allotted to men of eminence, or religious persons, to enable their maintenance. The *magtedar* was the owner of the land, and it was inherited by successive generations. *mutawalis* were expected to maintain the holy places and perform services out of the income of the land. The process of *zabti* was applicable to such grants also.

Muslims dominated administration in all the three classified areas. They were in majority in the administrative machinery, police, army, judiciary and other urban based elite services. The local Muslims here were totally dependent on government services or on similar jobs in the *jagirs*, subject to their satisfactory conduct. Those who were well educated were in high ranks whereas uneducated preferred being peons in the government or private offices. As a result the artisan group so prominent among the Muslims elsewhere was totally absent here. Muslims had no skill. They had Hindu butchers even for selling Halal muttan leave aside occupations like carpentry, barbery etc. Hindus got opportunities in village offices and in the rural economy. Agriculture was the major source of income and most fertile land was in the control of *Zamindars*. Apart from some government services, Hindus were also involved in farming, weaving, petty business in the rural areas, and in trade and industry in the urban areas.

Dominance in the service sector could not, however, prevent the majority of Muslims from being in a deprived economic position. In the prevailing feudal structure, a few nobles and *jagirdars* were the main beneficiaries of the system, enjoying an extremely luxurious life. Except depending on patty services (mostly clerical), Muslim masses were totally averse to agriculture, industry and business, and thus unlike the Hindus who were adept in the professions as well as commercial activities, could not generally be prosperous. Moneylending has also contributed to the prosperity of Hindus, and both, Muslims and Hindus, were under the strong grip of moneylenders. Population of the state was so divided that the Muslims concentrated in the city and district head-quarters dominating government services. The Hindus were majority in the villages, rural economy and in local revenue administration as *patels* and *patwaris*.

As Osman Ali Khan's rule progressed, Hindus were gradually becoming restive due to their exclusion from administration, though the two communites were still living in peace due to the impact of the composite culture and a relative absence of competitive conditions.

Politically, during the British rule, Hyderabad existed as an "independent" state, and a faithful ally of the British Government. Except foreign relations, the state had freedom to manage internal affairs without any intervention of the Viceroys of India. In 1857, the then Nizam of Hyderabad had secured the confidence of the British by not joining the freedom struggle and earlier, by supporting the British against Tipu Sultan, during the battle of Mysore, and finally, by contributing huge amounts to the British Government, whenever needed, as well as supplying manpower during the two world wars.

For internal purposes, Hyderabad state was independent in legislative, executive and judicial matters and the Nizam was the head of all the three agencies. Sources of revenue and the heads of expenditure were presented in the form of annual budget. The state had its own currency, postal and telegraphic services, railways, airways, and broadcasting system. Other public utility services such as mining, public construction services, water reservoirs and health services were organized on a state ownership basis. By increasing governmental activities, Hyderabad state had taken the shape of a welfare state during the period of the last Nizam (Ruler to Raj Pramukh).

There was a tradition that the Prime Minister would be appointed from amongst the feudals of Hyderadad and that too from the three feudal families—*Umra-e-Paigh*, Sir Salar Jung family and the Chandulal family. No one from outside the circle of Hyderabadi elites could ever be a minister. Mir Osman Ali Khan broke this tradition and appointed Sir Ali Imam from Bihar, Sir Akbar Hyderi from Bombay, Sir Mirza Ismail from Mysore and Nawab of Chhattari from U.P. as Prime Minister. Only Mir Laiq Ali, who was in the office at the time of Police Action, was from Hyderabad.

Administrative infrastructure was fully developed. Political theory of separation of powers was introduced in the year 1922 when the powers of executive and judiciary were separated. The efforts of Mir Osman Ali Khan to make Hyderabad a modern welfare state included the important step of introducing a new constitution in 1939 which sought to establish a parliamentary democracy, with Nizam as the Head of the state (Ruler to Raj Pramukh).

The state was lucky enough to have such a far-sighted ruler as well as very distinguished and able Prime Ministers such as Sir Saler Jung, Sir Ali Imam, Maharaja Kishan Parshad, Sir Akbar Hyderi, etc. who gave a sense of direction to the modernisation of the state. All of them tried their best to make administration more efficient and effective, and increased the sphere of public utility services. But the responsible positions were still confined to a few families of nobles. Recruitment policy was based on family background and proximity to royal or noble families. This social status-based recruitment concentrated administrative and social power into the hands of a small group. Recruitment to Hyderabad Civil Service, the highest administrative body of the state was restricted to members of the families of the nobles. This tradition had led to a sort of an oligarchy, in which the common people were in the position of an outcaste. Even after the establishment of Osmania University and spread of higher education the educated Muslims were also interested in *Mulazimat-e-Sarkar* (government service). Educated middle class Muslims became *Ahile-Kar* (clerks), and were quite content to having achieved their ambition. This has been rightly depicted in a couplet:

Kya kahin ahbab kya kare numayan kar gaye
B.A. kiya nukar huwe pension hoi aur mar gaye.

That is what our friends have ventured
graduation, employment, superannuation and death.

Bahadur Yar Jung tried to create interest in business and trade among the educated youth but he could not change the easy going nature of Hyderabadi Muslims,

On the positive side, the public works programmes of the Nizam were commendable and were beneficial to his subjects, due to which people felt grateful to their ruler. Some examples are illustrative. Hyderabad city had been the victim of floods before 1908 due to the uncontrolled flow of river Musi which had caused huge losses to life and property of citizens. A dam, named Osman Sagar, was constructed to control the flow; it saved the people from floods and increased the supply of drinking water to the city. Along with it, another dam known as Himayat Sagar was constructed. Besides these, many small irrigation projects, a big dam called Nizam Sagar Dam in district Nizamabad, were constructed to irrigate a large part of the Nizam's dominion. These measures were aimed at reducing dependency of agriculture on rainfall (*Financial Adviser*).

To spread education in the state Mir Osman Ali established a department of public instruction and started many primary, middle and high schools throughout the state. By establishing Osmania University in the year 1917 and a few colleges under its jurisdiction, higher education was promoted. In a report it was clearly stated that "the University roots would be firmly planted in oriental culture though they would also derive sustenance from western sciences and arts" (*Financial Adviser*).

Rail and road transport and a communication network was set up throughout the state with state funds. Among all the princely states of India, Hyderabad was the only state which had its own well-established railway system. The state was also air-linked with the other parts of India. A network of concrete roads was constructed through the city, and connected with different districts. Construction and maintenance of the roads was a continuous responsibility of the state and roads were well looked after (*Financial Adviser*).

There were also a number of public hospitals in existence in the city, as well as the district towns and villages where treatment was given free of charge. In the city, the Osmania General Hospital provided allopathic treatment, while the Sadar Unani Shafakhana offered treatment in *unani* system.

Water supply and drainage system were quite efficient in the city. Roads in the main city and in each locality were cleaned twice a day, in the morning and in the evening. The Hyderabad Municipal Corporation was responsible for all these activities. There was no concept of elected corporation, but it was a government department like any other. Many sites of public utility such as markets, gardens, parks, etc. were constructed. The public garden of Hyderabad was a centrally located and beautiful garden-cum-zoo of that time.

Since the very inception of the Cooperative Movement in India, cooperatives were established in the state. There was a separate government department to promote it. The state took special interest in strengthening the movement and providing facilities of loan to the farmers, along with a programme of rural reconstruction was also brought into effect. There was a Central Board for this purpose with branches in the districts and *talukas*. The purpose of this organization was to advise and create impetus among the farmers. A college of agriculture was also established to train personnel to modernize agriculture.

Historical monuments of Ellora and Ajanta, which are situated in Aurangabad, were well maintained under the supervision of two archaeologicalists from Italy and the Archaeological Department of Hyderabad. And it is rightly said "Even if all his other deeds are forgotten the Seventh Nizam is clearly entitled to the gratitude of posterity on this score alone". (Rajinder Prasad, 1984 : 17). The Department of Central Records kept records of century old documents and contracts. This material has been an important source for historians. There was a Bureau of Statistics which collected census statistics and other quantitative data concerning the state economy. For all these activities the last Nizam was known as the founder of modern Hyderabad.

3

Police Action and its Aftermath

When it became evident that the country was going to be divided into India and Pakistan, there was no alternative left for Hyderabad but to link its fate with the Indian Union. But the Nizam resisted this. As various acts of hostility on the border areas of the state by Congress Volunteers increased, the Razakars began to retaliate inside the state by looting and burning the houses of Hindus. The Government of India viewed these developments with grave concern and in order to resolve a ticklish problem was ready to relax the terms of accession for Hyderabad.

On 16th June 1948, it was announced on All India Radio that Hyderabad delegation had accepted the terms and conditions of accession and had taken the draft to Hyderabad for the Nizam's signature. Almost all the Muslim leaders and the Urdu Press of Hyderabad with rare exceptions, were supporting the demand of an independent state (*Rahberi Deccan*, 18th June, 1948).

As time passed by, both the border skirmishes and the internal situation deteriorated. The Hindu rural population became victim of organized attacks of *Razakars* and other armed Muslim criminals with the open collusion of the state police. A general atmosphere of fear and insecurity was spread among the Hindus, and they were subjected to various forms of harassment. Their loyalty was being questioned, houses were searched and valuables were taken away, crushing any resistance. Panic stricken Hindus rushed across the borders, and migrated to safer areas in India. In the Muslim perception, however, the *Razakars* were champions of the Muslim cause and were credited as the defenders of an independent Hyderabad.

Ironically, it was not obvious to the Muslim community that the state was heading towards a disaster, though the more balanced Muslims raised their voices against all this. They were against Qasim Rizvi (the President of the Majlis), his policies and the atrocities of the *Razakars.* But they could not come out openly as they feared being killed or their houses ransacked and their family members tortured. Hence their pretext was a feeble one.

A statement signed by twelve Muslim intellectuals describing the deterioration of the law and order situation in the state, and the *Razakars,* atrocities on Hindus in the districts was published in a Urdu newspaper (*Payam.* 13th August, 1948). The same statement was also publishin be another newspaper 'Imroze'. It evoked a ready response from sensible Muslims. But it was severely criticised and, Shoebullah Khan, the editor of 'Imroze' was assassinated. On the whole, the Urdu press played damaging and one-sided communal role in that entire period. To give an example, when on the 4th of September, 1948, Baqar Ali Mirza (A famous Congress leader of Hyderabad) had issued a statement criticising the state government and the *Razakars,* he pointed out that they were not doing any service to the state by alienating such a large section of the people and operating as the puppcts of the Muslim League. This statement could not be published in any newspaper (Farid Mirza, 1976).

Cousequently, the communal harmony that existed between the Hindus and Muslims in the past began to melt away, and the Hindus lost their confidence in the Muslims ; a point of "no return" was reached. It became evident to the Government of India that there was not going to be any solution to the problem of the integration of Hyderabad state into India on the basis of negotiations. The Police Action finally was initiated by the Government of India on 13th September, 1948.

The basis on which the Indian Army marched into Hyderabad state, was that the law and order situation had deteriorated and the life and property of the Hindus, who formed the numerical majority was in danger. The Muslims had no way of assessing the damage caused by the lawlessness of the *Razakars*. They had been both blind and deaf towards reality. An idea of their fool hardiness can be had from the fact that just prior to Police Action, Qasim Rizvi appointed himself the Field Marshal and in a number of speeches and press statements, he assured the Muslim masses that the yellow Asaf Jahi flag would soon be flying atop the Red Fort in Delhi (*Rahberi Deccan*, from June to Sept. 1948).

On 17th September Qasim Rizvi addressed the people of Hyderabad on Hyderabad Radio. He said "there are rumours in the city that I have escaped away to Pakistan. I am born in Deccan and shall be buried here. I have lived with you and will die with you. I have taken the first drop of your blood but shall not take the last drop. Whatever may be the consequences of the situation, please face them and endure. It is the will of God, and we the people of Hyderabad should accept it". (*Deccan Chronicle*, 18 Sept. 1948).

After this emotional peroration he came out of the Radio Station and saluted the Asaf Jahi flag on the building for the last time, and left in his car. People around him burst into tears. This incident has been reported by one of the informants who was an eye witness.

The same evening the Nizam also addressed his people from Radio Hyderabad and declared that the state of Hyderabad had merged with the Indian Union. He appealed to the citizens to be peaceful and cooperate with the military administration under Major General J.N. Chaudhry.

On the 18th September though the Indian army had not yet arrived in the city, there was panic among the Muslims as Hyderabad had surrendered. Despite heavy rains large number of Hindus were roaming on the streets shouting "Pandit Nehru ki Jai", "Sardar Patel ki Jai". This was something unexpected for the Muslims who were all shocked and demoralised beyond description. Their leaders had promised to conquer Red Fort, but in fact they had lost whatever they had. In a matter of just five days, the glory and splendour of centuries had been ruined. Had the integration been done in a peaceful way, the Muslims would not have encountered embarrassment at the hands of Hindus who felt victorious. The Government of India was prepared to give special concessions to the state of Hyderabad but the intellectual bankruptcy of the Muslim leadership had prevented them from seizing these concessions. Some of the educated Hindus were of the view that the showdown was in the interests of majority community, otherwise thc Muslims would have remained under the false notions of their untested strength (speeches of Hindu leaders of Hyderabad, *Deccan Chronicle*, Sept. 20th to Oct. 30th, 1948).

Apart from what the newspapers and magazines had reported about the Police Action, there is virtually no systematic account available of the human dimension of this unfortunate event. In the perspective of larger national interest the Police Action was, no doubt, imminent and inevitable. But for the Muslims of Hyderabad, especially in the context of immediacy it was a tragedy of the greatest proportions ; it was a tragedy that bore a similarity of kind if not of scale with the collapse of the Mughal empire in Delhi. For Hyderabadi Muslims who had lived through those fateful days, it was a trauma that they could never forget till their last breath.

With the passage of time memories of such events fade away from the minds of the people, but are not totally wiped away. Therefore, the researcher thought it worthwhile to obtain personal accounts from the informants selected for this study, in order to build up an exponential account (though long delayed) of trauma.

According to the informants though the Indian Army did not resort to any violence in the city of Hyderabad, yet there were innumerable incidents of looting of houses and property as well as large scale killing of Muslims. These cases were particularly noticed in those districts from where the Indian military had entered Hyderabad state. Hyderabad city itself saw less of Hindu atrocities. The presence of Indian army provided the local Hindus a good opportunity to satisfy their thirst for revenge of all that the *Razakars* had done to them. This was, in a way, a blessing in disguise, because the sieged Muslims from the rural areas of affected districts rushed for refuge and safety to the city. Some of the rural Muslims ran into the jungles leaving behind their homes and property. Thus it was the Muslims of the outlying districts like Osmanabad, Aurangabad, Bidar, Nanded and Parbhani who bore the brunt of the Police Action.

Though the *Razakars* had sown the seeds but the entire community had to reap the harvast of hatred and hostility. Widespread grabbing of Muslim property and indiscriminate killing became the order of the day. In addition, there were mass arrests of Muslims on the accusation that they were *Razakars* ; in fact, any Muslim could be arrestea and put behind bars on this ground. (In the researcher's own family such examples were found).

It was also reported by informants that the new administration suspended/dismissed many Muslim officers on charges of negligence/corruption during and after the Police Action. A list of some three hundred government officers who had been dismissed on such charges was published by the government. Any Muslim officer wanting to dispose of his property had to first obtain a clearance from the government. The officials appointed to grant this permission were ideally placed to earn fabulous bribes. In addition, tribunals consisting of three members one each from the military, the government and the university were constituted to look into the excesses that were committed before the Police Action. These tribunals had unlimited authority and could even award capital punishment without any appeal against their decision (Ramesan, ed., 1966).

Arrests and suspension of Muslims continued even one year after Police Action. Each arrest disheartened other officers and motivated/compelled them to escape to Pakistan. In course of time the military administrator General J.N. Chaudhary respeatedly promised that a list of officers against whom there were charges would be notified so that the others could live peacefully. But the list never did get released and many innocent officers were harassed. The informants added that it was one way of deliberately compelling Muslim officers to migrate to Pakistan.

Disturbed by the accounts of tyranny perpetrated upon the Muslims, the Government of India appointed the Pandit Sunderlal Commission in 1951 to assess the situation and to report to the Government. At least according to one account Pandit Sunderlal a socialist leader is said to have wept upon seeing the sufferings of the Muslims. In a confidential report to Prime Minister Nehru he wrote, "It has been proved that what was done after Police Action was much more than what had been done before" (*Rehnumae Deccan*, 8th Nov. 1951).

In this hour of reckoning (it was mentioned during the investigation) Muslims throughout Hyderabad state were burdened with a sense of guilt and loss and there was some heart searching as to why this fate had befallen them. As reported by the respondents, the *Roomi Topi* or the fez cap and the *sherwani* disappeared overnight. Even those Muslims who had not participated in the *Razakar* movement at all or those who had opposed the movements were also afraid of the onslaught on the community. Almost all the newspapers of those days raised their voice against the en mass arrests of innocent people without even giving them a chance to appeal in the court of law. Now that the centre of the *Razakars* had been paralysed and they were in no position to harm anyone, these arrests and detentions were meaningless. But when revenge is sought, such considerations are immaterial.

Many promises made by responsible Congressmen like B. Ram Krishnan Rao that "Muslims in services will not be harassed by interrogations", (Fareed Mirza, 1976) could not be kept. The suspensions, dismissals and arrests of the Muslim officers and the confiscation of their property led them into an acute financial crisis. There was a general dissatisfaction among Muslims regarding the insufficient and mismanaged relief work. A letter written by a civil servant to the Government of Hyderabad gives an idea of the grimness of the situation (see Appendix).

Inevitably, the Urdu Press highlighted the plight of the Muslims. This is illustrated by the following examples. Some extracts from the Urdu Press, June, 1949 are as under :

(1) "Even nine months after Police Action, violence continued and the number of Muslim widows and orphans kept on increasing. In most of the reported cases four to five members of each family were murdered. There were mothers whose two or three sons, and in some cases the only son, were dragged out of their homes and killed. Even children were not spared. The killings in most of the cases were organized." (Editorial : *Rahnuma-i-Deccan*, 20 June, 1949).

(2) "Muslim property was under the illegal occupation of the Hindu goondas. The government's attitude was apathetic. Photographs of the damaged property and merciless killings have been published in the press. Goondas have got an impression that the administration was with them and they could do whatever they wanted with the Muslims." (*Rahnuma-i-Deccan*, 2nd June, 1949).

(3) "In many villages there were only widows left without even a single man, young or old. Some of the officers deputed in these areas were taking an undue advantage of such a situation." (*Payam*, 10th June, 1949).

Some of the informants stated that even though they were officers they were retired compulsorily and their pensions were not sanctioned for a very long time. Deliberate negligence and lack of attention to Muslims' complaints prevailed universally. But notwithstan ding this depressing situation, some informants categorically mentioned a few examples which showed that some of the illiterate Hindus betrayed humanitarian feelings and saved the lives of several Muslims at the cost of their own, and provided the latter with food and shelter for many days.

After the Police Action and the reorganisation of the state, Hindu-Muslim relations entered into a phase of adjustment to the new situation, With the lessening of Nizam's influence and disappearance of his patronage, the Muslims were under pressure to develop a new approach and attitude. The end of Nizam's supremacy resulted in the decline of the dominance of Muslims in those sectors of employment in which they had enjoyed a monopoly, for generations. Abolition of *jagirs*, introduction of land reforms, democratization of services, disbandment of Hyderabad army and Nizam's irregulars and many such factors led to unemployment among the Muslims.

Another factor responsible for Muslim unemployment was their proficiency in Urdu, Arabic and Persian instead of English. As the state language no more remained Urdu, several employees in government service were given premature retirement.

All this forced upon the Muslims an inferior social position. For the first time they encountered a feeling of insecurity and a loss of identity leading to a state of psychological alienation. The trauma of political and social powerlessness was so intense as to leave the community dumb with shock. This is shown by the fact that no creative writings appeared for almost three decades except such writings as expressed the anguish of lost power and glory. Recently, with financial recovery due to petrodollars, Hyderabadi Muslims have started expressing their experiences of the past turmoil.

(1) *Socio-Economic Problems of Muslims after Police Action* : Soon after the fall of Nizam's Kingdom the *Jagir* Abolition Regulation was implemented in 1949. Following this the Muslim elite was deprived of its special privileges, feudal prerogatives and preferential treatment.

Besides *jagir* abolition, some other changes also adversely affected the common Muslims who were totally dependent on government service. Generally the government jobs did not provide very lucrative salaries, yet there was contentment even with low paid jobs as income was assured, and as these jobs gave the Muslims a sense of being partners in running the government.

After Police Action, there was heavy retrenchment of Muslims from civil, military and judicial services. Many of the old government departments like customs were totally abolished. Nizam's regular and irregular troops were disbanded. Some of these steps were perhaps considered inevitable to reshape the administration.

Jagirdars and other private employees of the Nizam who became disinherited and impoverished in their turn, dismissed many of their personal and official servants.

According to Khusro's work (1956) on *Jagirdari* Abolition and Land Reforms in Hyderabad, 11-15% of the Muslim population of the state was adversely affected, three quarters of which resided in about a dozen urban centres. Furthermore, nearly half of the population of the city of Hyderabad depended for its livelihood on five major categories of employment. Five of these were inextricably linked with the feudal set-up. These categories were :

(1) *Jagirs*, *Mansabs* and *Inams*.

(2) Employment in government and quasi-government departments and establishment—revenue offices, civil and judicial offices, Police, Municipality and City Improvement Board, education and university service.

(3) Army, regular and Nizam irregulars (*fouj-e-begaida*).

(4) Offices of the feudal estates and household establishments of the feudal gentry.

(5) Private service with aristocratic families; and

(6) Professions other than government service such as lawyers, physicians, engineers and business (Rasheeduddin Khan, 1971).

During the Nizam's period many Urdu knowing persons notwithstanding low qualifications (such as matric pass/fail and even middle school fail) were in government service in clerical and other menial jobs. They were compulsorily retired after Police Action, and their vacancies were filled by younger people with better qualifications but were not from the Muslim community. Thus, a chain of joblessness was set into motion.

Then again, there was a sizeable section of lawyers, who, with short term training, used to serve the needs of the judicial system of the state. Just one year's course of 'law class' enabled them to practice in any court of Hyderabad in revenue, civil and criminal matters. There was practically no pre-requisite qualification to join this course except a good command of Urdu language. All these lawyers were replaced by regular law graduates, due to the introduction of English language in the courts.

All this adversely affected the economic condition of the Muslims. The crisis became particularly acute because, with the few exceptions, the majority of Muslims were entirely dependent on government services. They were not interested in business or commerce, did not dominate any special occupations, nor had developed any occupational skills that would have made them self-reliant. As a result, they became all the more helpless in the changing situation. It was a situation of abject dejection leading withdrawal and resignation. This also pushed them more and more into the world of religion and fatalism. Many of them considered their plight as a punishment from God due to their immoral recklessness.

The situation within the first five years of Police Action was more miserable. Countless victims had poured into the city from the adjoining districts and villages. Many of the male members became rickshaw pullers or hawkers. Many of the women were pushed into prostitution. A considerable number of people, particularly those with a questionable political record, left for Pakistan.

An index of the near destitution level reached by certain section of the Muslim community in Hyderabad is provided by four revealing surveys conducted by the Indian Institute of Economics, Hyderabad.

(1) The major conclusions of "A Socio-Economic Survey of Rickshaw Drivers in Hyderabad City Areas", Hyderabad (1962), conducted on a systematic random survey basis are as follows :

(a) Of the 16,708 rickshaw pullers, the proportion of Muslims to non-Muslims among owner-drivers was 9 : 1 and among drivers is 2 : 1.

(b) Daily hire-wage was between Rs. 1.25 to Rs. 2.00, i.e. Rs. 37.50 to Rs. 60.00 per month and daily earnings varied between Rs. 2.50 and Rs. 5.00, i.e. Rs. 75 to Rs. 150 per month.

(c) Average size of the family of Muslim rickshaw puller was 5-6.

(d) Literacy ratio at 47 : 32 was higher among Muslims than non-Muslims.

(e) The occupational pattern of Muslims prior to taking to rickshaw pulling was as follows: 28.2% ex-employees in the Nizam's estate, 19.5% unemployed, 14.5% casual employees, 10.4% skilled workers, 5.9% retail traders and 14.3% others.

(2) "A Socio-Ecomic Survey of Street Beggars in Hyderabad" (1956) revealed that in a total of appoximately 5,000 beggars, Muslims constituted 48%, that is, even more than the scheduled castes. The main reasons for this proportion, the survey team reported, were the 'Police Action', Abolition of *Jagirs* and disbandment of the regular and irregular forces (Report on a "Socio-Economic and Health Survey of Street Beggars in Hyderabad—Secundrabad City Area", Hyderabad, 1956).

(3) "A Socio-Economic Survey of Hut-Dwellers of Hyderabad City" (1959) also conducted as a random sample survey reported that 67,806 persons constituting 8% of city's population lived in 21,842 huts, while 53% of the hutment dwellers belonged to the scheduled castes, 24.9% were Muslims and only 1.07% from among Christians.

(4) "Bulletin of the Hyderabad Metropolitan Project" (1966) stated that southern Hyderabad "the walled city" where three-quarters of the Muslim population lived, was weak in all the three measures of urbanisation, i.e., proportion of working population, existence of manufacturing industries and commercial activities.

Although the loss of power was equally shocking for all the three classes, but each class showed a differential response. Interviews with the informants and the family history record of the respondents revealed that the worst vicitms of Police Action were the upper class and the lower class Muslims.

For the aristocratic families it was not easy to reconcile to the loss of inherited wealth and power, which they had enjoyed for generations. However, the response in this class was not uniform. Those elites who were holding high positions merely on the basis of their family background found themselves totally ruined, and entered a permanent phase of stagnation and decline. But those aristocrats who were well-equipped with higher education, after the initial set-back gradually succeeded in regaining their old social position, and continue to be the privileged class. Examples are Zahir Ahmed, Naseeruddin Hashmi, Hashim Amir Ali, Ali Yawar Jung, Sadat Ali Khan, Zainyar Jung, Mohiuddin Qadri Zor, etc.

For the middle class too Police Action was a great trauma. But for obvious reasons, it was not so profoundly destabilizing for families in this strata as in the upper class with the disintegration of the feudal order. Notwithstanding the new government's discriminatory policies, meritorious Muslims did get recognition, and according to our informants, middle class Muslims realized that in the new set-up their hardwork and competition would not go waste. Perhaps it was for the first time that they got a chance to show their calibre and be suitably rewarded irrespective of their family background. Apprehensions of discriminatory attitude by the new government made them realise that the only way to survive was throuch hardwork and competition. The consequence of this realization was that they realised the importance of higher education, particularly of professional education. This change began to open the doors of high government position and other avenues to the more meritorious middle class Muslims. This was a new dimension in social change which would not have been possible in feudal set-up, despite a Muslim government. However, such instances were not too many. Quite a large number of people finding themselves in a disadvantageous position under the new dispensation migrated to Pakistan and to western countries.

These migrations, in the long run, proved to be a blessing in disguise. Those Muslim students who could not secure a job after obtaining a university degree, found avenues of employment because of the opportunities abroad. This contained a great deal of frustration of the Muslim middle class. Furthermore, when the middle class youth perceived employment opportunities abroad, its efforts in studying hard and doing well in the examinations were intensified. Parents too were willing to sacrifice and support foreign education of their wards. Thus in an unanticipated way, the trials and tribulations faced by the middle class got converted into a blessing.

The lower class neither sensitive enough to experience the tragedy nor did it have the far-sightedness to realize that the need of the hour was to work hard, and better equip itself to earn out a decent living. After a dependency on the elites, for several generations, individuals in this class were unambitious, apathetic and easy going, had no occupational skills to earn a living, and could only fall upon begging, domestic service and prostitution, which many of them adopted.

It has been indicated in this chapter that following the Police Action, initially upper class individuals, and subsequently middle class youth also, went to the western countries for education. As has been the case with many Indians, Hyderabadi Muslims also settled down in large numbers along with their families in the more hospitable and opportunity laden countries like England, USA, Canada, etc. In what follows we deal with this migration.

Migrations have always been very rewarding in the history of Hyderabad. In the previous chapters it has already been observed that Muslims from all over India had migrated to Hyderabad after the mutiny of 1857 (and continued to be so until 1947), due to it being the most prosperous Muslim state of its times, and could therefore provide refuge to the immigrant Muslims fleeing from north India. But ironically the Police Action in 1948 reversed direction of migration and Hyderabadi Muslims for the first time in history, were now forced to migrate out of the state. Emigration was now their escape route. Rather than face the situation of role reversal, large numbers of those Muslims who came from U.P. and Bihar at the time of mutiny, decided to quit the state, alongwith a few Hyderabadi Muslims with questionable political records.

Prior to Police Action, upper class and middle class Hyderabadi Muslims had been content with their life situations. The feudal set-up had produced an opiating effect on their minds and they could not be motivated to go anywhere in the world even if such a movement involved improvement in prospects. If circumstances did require a short visit out of Hyderabad, the send off was often turned into a kind of social event. Not only family members but even distant relatives gathered to see the individuals off. They prayed for his safe travel and tied *Imam-e-Zamin* (coins stitched in coloured and embroided strips of cloth) on the arm for his safe journey. Upon his return home, these coins were given away to beggars as charity. Indeed, even within the state, mobility from rural areas to Hyderabad city were not very common. People generally stayed rooted to their ancestral homes, families, kinsmen and friends. The stagnation in geographical and spatial mobility was finally dissolved by the trauma of Police Action. The political upheaval of 1948 pushed people far beyond their homes and hearths. Reconstructing the scale of migrations on the basis of data collected from the informants, it would appear that three important factors motivated migrations in the years following 1948; these were political, economic and educational. Each of these factors predominated in different periods.

(2) *Migration to Pakistan* : Data in this connection has been collected from immediate family members, that is, parents or siblings.

The first phase of emigration to Pakistan started just after Police Action in September 1948, which had shocked Hyderabadi Muslims as nothing had ever shocked them before in their memory. Unable to read the writing on the wall, Hyderabadi Muslims had lived in an unreal world, not realising that a Muslim ruler could ever submit to "Hindu India". Their psychological unpreparedness for such a calamity is evident from the government's *farmans* (Royal proclamations issued till the eve of Police Action) which used to include the following clause in Urdu :

Ta Qayam-e-Shams-o-Qamar (meaning, "till the revolutions of the sun and moon").

By implication this meant that the Nizam's rule would last until this world of ours would last.

The military government under the supervision of Major General J. N. Chaudhary, on 19th September 1948, registered a number of cases against the *Razakars* and a massive hunt was started to arrest them. This spread panic among the Muslims and they started realizing that they had no future in Hyderabad. As was to be expected, those Muslims who were in high position in the Nizam's army and civil services opted for Pakistan. Among those who migrated were Prime Minister Laiq Ali and cabinet ministers like Yamin Zubairi, Abdur Raouf, Abdur Rahim and secretaries to the government, etc. (In fact, Laiq Ali escaped under somewhat dramatic circumstances, not unlike the escape of Shivaji from Aurangzeb's court). Among the middle class migrants to Pakistan were the *Razakar* activists who had spearheaded the movement against India, and who therefore had no other alternative. Besides, most north Indian families who had settled in Hyderabad in order to benefit from the opportunities it afforded when it was a Muslim state, left for Pakistan when Muslim supremacy came to an end in the state.

Two facts however are noteworthy. First, the Nizam himself decided to stay back as a citizen of Indla after handing over his power to the Indian government which, however, showed no vindictiveness and appointed him the *Raj Pramukh*. Second, notwithstanding the nervousness and gloom that had seized Hyderabadi Muslims, there was no large scale exodus to Pakistan. Only a section of the elites and the political activists left. Possibly the Nizam's decision to stay on in India and the Nehru government's attitude of 'forgive and forget' helped restore confidence. Thus barring those who knew that they would be uncomfortable in the new set-up, the ordinary Muslims, by and large, decided to stay back and face the consequences. One exception, here, was that of rural Muslims who had been so dazed by the atrocities of the post-Police Action period, that they decided to begin life afresh in Pakistan, rather than return to their village homes or stay on in the city. The collected data from family histories indicates this. Possibly, the relatively low migration was due to the traditional strong attachment to the land. Many of the respondents said that had the Nizam opted for Pakistan, the migration would have definitely been of a larger magnitude.

Another important point reported by the informants was that in the case of Deccani Muslims only one or two members of each family migrated leaving behind the rest of the family. These migrants were either in military or police departments or civil services or actively involved in the *Razakar* movements. But in the case of those who were from U.P. and had settled in Hyderabad prior to Pakistan, the tendency was to migrate to Pakistan *in toto*.

Informants and those respondents who remember incidents of migration to Pakistan recalled with mixed feelings the events of those days. To aggravate the plight of the Muslims came the Evacuee Property Act, introduced in 1948. It was implemented so ruthlessly that even if a single member from a family owning property migrated to Pakistan, the entire property was confiscated by the government, and those left behind were left penniless. Many families were greatly affected by this and got involved in endless law suits to save their property from seizure. Tragically, while those who stayed behind had to pay a penalty, those who migrated soon after the Police Action received substantial compensation in Pakistan. The migration to Pakistan continued till the mid 1950s.

Migration of the middle class individuals or families to Pakistan was no easy task. Informants related pathetic stories of the uprooting of such persons. Besides the emotional trauma that parting involved and dear ones the parents and others left behind were totally ignorant of the whereabouts of their dear ones, they left Hyderabad. Postal services between India and Pakistan were not at all satisfactory. Those who had reached Pakistan would not write their actual experiences because the letters were censored.

Migrants to Pakistan, however, even after settling down were not in a position to help family members whom they had left behind in Hyderabad due to the restrictions imposed on the transfer of money to India. Partly due to this, and partly because life for Muslims in Hyderabad gradually began to settle down, the outflow of migrants to Pakistan was to a limited extent. Majority of the Muslims remained behind to compromise and adjust to the new situation even though for quite some time many families faced difficult times. The attachment to one's roots and native soil, however, has often triumphed in human history against heavy odds. In the case of Hyderabad, too, eventually the tragedy of Police Action was to motivate and help Muslims overcome their unhappy condition. Once they came to terms with reality, they learned to adjust to it and came out of their false pride and self-deception, and began to get into various professions, accepted many skilled and unskilled jobs, and thus began to build a new world for themselves, a world which was to be different from the feudel set-up that now lay completely shattered. Of course, they had to face many adversities but in the process of challenging adversities, a new kind of self-confidence was born in the community and gradually, even before the decade of the fifty's was over, migrations to Pakistan began to diminish to a point at which they became insignificant. (This was not so in north India where migrations to Pakistan were to continue until the time of the Bangladesh war.)

(3) *Migration to West* (*U.K., U.S.A., Canada and West Germany*) : Migration of Hyderabadi Muslims to western countries also needs to be studied carefully. Qualitatively and quantitatively, this migration was different from that to Pakistan. Going to western countries for higher education had been quite popular, since a long time, among the upper classes of the Muslim society of Hyderabad. Outstanding students from elite families were sent to England for higher studies by the government of Hyderabad. There were also a few examples of some well-to-do families sending their wards abroad on their own expenses. Some ambitious and well-off

middle class Muslim youth also managed to go abroad. Even after the establishment of Osmania University a foreign degree was very much in vogue. But following Police Action all those who could afford to go abroad began to prefer western universities to Osmania. This was so because foreign education became an escape mechanism both against the psychologically intolerable conditions in Hyderabad as well as from discriminations in admission in Osmania University.

Thus the period of the 1950s and early 1960s saw young Muslims heading towards American, British and German Universities. From among those who went, a considerable majority stayed back permanently in the western countries and took their families with them after disposing of their property in Hyderabad. However some of the graduates did return and got absorbed in various government departments or in the various professions. Consequently, in contrast to the general situation of Muslims in India, quite a few Hyderabadi Muslims are today among the top medical practitioners, engineers, architects and university teachers of the city and enjoy the patronage mostly of a Hindu clientele. (Apart from the University town of Aligarh, Hyderabad is the only city in India with so many educated Muslims.)

The individuals who were successful in establishing themselves abroad and shifting their families proved to be a good source of inspiration for many distant relatives ; seeing their example, other young people in such families looked towards migration to the west as their greatest ambition in life. They got the inspiration to work hard and get good results in their studies at home. Once undergraduate studies were completed, efforts to migrate gained momentum. In fact, young students from rich families were sent to western universities even for undergraduate studies. Since their families could afford—to do so. The desire to go abroad had now become so intense, that in middle class families parents were willing to incur loans or sell off their property in order to send their children for further education. In some cases youths who were more enterprising themselves sought loans from banks for this purpose.

Those who took up permanent residence abroad, maintained links with Hyderabad. Just as Londoners, Parsians and Lucknowites have been proud of their city and culture, Hyderabadis too are extremely fond of their city, and can never tear themselves completely away from it. From time to time these foreign settled Hyderabadis return home in vacations to meet their relations or attend marriages etc. Usually, at the behest of parents, they also came back to marry Hyderabadi girls. Their only condition while marrying was preference for convent educated girls. Such schooling thus became a very important factor in the subsequent migration of Hyderabadi Muslim girls.

The possibility of migration to west helped the Muslims of Hyderabad in their aspirations of upward mobility. This was particularly so in the case of middle class young men. Indeed, in course of time they were able to move ahead educationally, occupationally and financially of those traditional elites who had been less venturesome and had stayed back in the city or the country.

Furthermore, migration to the west also had a profound socio-psychological impact. Western education, as has already been pointed out elsewhere, had, in feudal times, been the virtual monopoly of the elite families. But now middle class parents were also proud of their children's achievements abroad. In social gatherings they talked of their sons with a sense of pride. As for the youth, a way out had been found, and there came a new-found confidence for a bright future.

Exposure to the western society was a challenging experience for such Hyderabadi youth as were the product of a feudal society. For the first time there started a self-supporting family life which compelled the people to shed their pretensions of false prestige ; in the equalitarian west, they learned to work for their survival, and understood the meaning of dignity of labour. But at the same time such an exposure to the economic order in the western society made people money minded. The feudal society of Hyderabad which was for a very long time under the influence of the

British feudal system culturally, now came under the impact of cheap Americanism in the name of modernisation.

Regarding their attitude towards returning to their homeland, it generally depended upon their class, social status and prestige in society. Youth of those elite families, which remained influential even in the politics of the new social set-up were least reluctant to come back and, on their return were, in fact, placed in high ranking jobs. But the youth of those families who were no better than the commoners and had lost all their influence and status were keen in shifting their families abroad. In case of the middle class youth, they did not return to their homeland willingly, those who returned to Hyderabad did it only on the insistence of their parents. It was perhaps a natural parental desire to see their children prosper in their native place so that they could take some pride in the prosperity and achievements of their children. For them it was more satisfying and prestigious to be known as a father of the foreign-returned-son rather than enjoyinglong term benefit by letting their sons stay in the lands of opportunities. Informants reported certain examples where the middle class youth refused to return in spite of their parents' insistence. While the young preferred to stay abroad, their parents took it to be very callous on the part of the younger generation to behave in that manner. There were certain examples reported when the sons could not see their parents even in the last moments of their lives and their desire remained unfulfilled.

Independent migration of women to the west was considerably low. And whatever cases of migration were reported they were through marriage. Parents of girls were found to be more keen and ethusiastic to find such a match. Dowry proved to be a very important consideration. As discussed in most of the middle class families it was the brides' parents who financed their spouses' visits abroad.

Now the researcher came across a few middle class families who had settled down in the U.S.A. in the late fifties and had come on their visit to the homeland in search of a suitable match for their children. In spite of their stay for about two decades they still wanted that their children should marry Hyderabadi girls. They appeared to be quite biased against the exposure of their daughters to the western culture. Such parents fixed up the marriages of their daughters with well-educated promising young men preferably with a degree in engineering or medicine. It is generally through marriages that the youth in Hyderabad are migrating to west.

The informants reported that those families which had settled down in the western countries, when they visited their homeland were found to be more religious minded and practising Muslims as compared to those staying in Hyderabad.

4

Overseas Employment

Under this heading, it is proposed to examine social change occurring among the Muslims of Hyderabad due to the inflow of petrodollars. Data for this was collected on the basis of interviews with the informants, and this was supplemented by the researcher's own observations in the course of her field work.

Since the beginning of the 1970, the oil boom of the West Asian countries opened up the doors of opportunities to the people of all the countries of the world.

Indians, in their lakhs, also took advantage of the situation. According to 1981 census, the highest number of emigrants to West Asia were from Kerala, while Andhra Pradesh stood second. It was estimated in a survey (Majeedul Hasan, 1982) that there were about one lakh persons from Hyderabad city working in different countries, and 95% of them were Muslims. Certain historical factors helped Hyderabadi Muslims to find economic opportunities in the Gulf states. It would be useful to consider these historical links in order to get a proper background regarding the specially advantageous position in which Hyderabadi Muslims found themselves when opportunity knocked at their door.

(1) *The Arab Connection*: Since 1803, it had been a tradition with the various Nizams of Hyderabad to recruit Arabs from such countries as Saudi Arabia, Somalia, Yaman, Qutar etc. Arab soldiers were entrusted with duties of guarding palaces and harems. The Arab generals commanded very

high respect and were considered very loyal and brave, and were conferred titles of honour, as a reward of their loyalty. All the male babies of Arab families were entitled to certain monetary payment from the very day they were born. These babies, upon growing up were expected to join the special Arab regiment, known as "Nizam-e-Jamiat".

Besides this royal patronage, the local Muslims also had great respect for the Arabs because they hailed from the sacred land of Mecca and spoke Arabic, the language of Quran. The Arabs enjoyed this position till Hyderabad state became a part of Indian union in 1948. Even at the time of Police Action the commander-in-chief of the Nizam's army was an Arab-Habeeb-Al-Idrus. Due to this prestige and popularity Arabs in their thousands were attracted to Hyderabad; over the years a large number of them came to Hyderabad and settled down here. A good reason for the Arab influx to Hyderabad was that during the time the Arab lands were not at all affluent, while Hyderabad on the other hand was. The Nizam's reputation as the richest man on earth was widely known, particularly among Muslims.

When the Arabs first came and settled in Hyderabad they were very particular about their ethnic identity and avoided marrying non-Arabs. But with the passage of time they overcame this inhibition and started marrying local Muslim women. These marriage alliances were homogamous in nature i.e. the superior rank Arab officers married among the local noble families, while the families of soldiers of lower rank got married into families that were below the native nobility. In this way, intermarriage led to the assimilation of the Arabs into the social fabric of Hyderabadi Muslim society.

The Arab chiefs used to live in big mansions with great pomp and show; some of these still exist as relics of that era. While the chiefs resided in elite localities, the lower ranked soldiers were concentrated in one particular locality, known as 'Barkas'; it was from this barkas locality that the initial migrations to the Gulf countries in search of overseas employment began.

From the informants it was learnt that prior to the oil boom in the Kingdom of Saudi Arabia, the Nizams of Hyderabad, particularly the last Nizam, used to send donations to the Saudi government, especially to help the poverty stricken people there. The common Muslims of Hyderabad appreciated this generosity of the Nizams. Occasionally, other well-to-do Hyderabadi Muslims also used to collect funds on their own and send them to Mecca. A leading Muslim businessman, Allauddin, established a trust to send regular financial donations to Saudi Arabia. A multi-storeyed shopping complex was constructed by Allauddin in the heart of the city, at Pathargatti, in the 1940s—called Madina Building, whose entire rent was donated to Saudi Arabia for charity purposes. Such actions had generated a lot of goodwill among the Arabs, and helped create a favourable climate for job opportunities for the Muslims of Hyderabad when affluence began to smile upon the Arabs.

The VII Nizam of Hyderabad, Mir Osman Ali Khan, continued his favours towards the Arab community even after he lost his monarchy. He continued to adopt some of the Arab babies (both girls and boys), who were called *Khana-zadi* and *khana-zad*. These were actually the children of the Arab army officers who had lost their jobs due to the disbandment of his army. These *khana-zadi* were brought up in the Royal Palace and were married to *khana-zad.* They were allotted separate residences in front of the King Kothi (the Royal Palace). All their needs were taken care of by the Nizam, and food was provided to them three times a day from the Royal kitchen.

The researcher in her young age, was a witness to scenes in the 1960s in which she used to observe huge trays of lavish breakfast, lunch and dinner being carried from the Royal kitchen to the *khanazada* residences. Each would be covered with yellow coloured beautifully embroided cloth called *torepash,* while the covered tray was called *khan.*

The institution of *khana-zadi* (khana-house, and zada-son) came into existence around the 1950s when it became unbearable for the Nizam to remain contended with a commoner's social status, without anyone to salute and pay respect to "His Majesty". So in order to satisfy his ego he started this institution. Eventually, these *khana-zadi* became very close to the Nizam, and were trusted by him to a greater extent than the local people of Hyderabad, who had once been his subjects. He treated them as his family members, whenever a new baby was born he would visit the newly born and deposit ten thousand rupees in the name of each baby in the bank.

The Nizam continued such favours towards the Arab community till his last breath. But in spite of all these favours, not all members of Hyderabad's Arab community benefited from the Nizam's favours. A majority of them had suffered greatly after the Police Action. The Hyderabad state army was disbanded in 1952, with a part of its being merged with the Indian army. For obvious reasons the Arab officers and soldiers could not be absorbed when the merger took place, and therefore became demobilized. Since many of them were not well educated they were not qualified enough to get absorbed into any other service. Consequently, for fifteen to twenty years they had to face a very difficult period. Most of them grew fruits and sold them on their bicyles, or even accepted petty jobs as *chowkidars*, etc. The local name for these Arabs was *Chaoush*. Several *chaoush* were seen on the main roads as well as in different localities selling fruits. They were special favourites of the children who enjoyed their peculiar accent and dress.

Interviews with the informants revealed that the struggle for survival of these Arabs continued till the dawn of the oil bonanza in the Gulf countries. Prosperity in the Gulf region encouraged the Arabs of Hyderabad to renew their ties with their ancestral lands. They started returning to their original homelands, claiming citizenship there. On settling down, they started obliging their Hyderabadi friends in sending visas for them. In course of time, the possibility of arranging of visas was to generate lucrative business for those with right contacts. This opportunity was seized by the Hyderabadi Muslims many of whom were better educated than most Arabs.

The initial stream of migrations in course of time became a huge tidal wave and countless Hyderabadis found lucrative jobs and reversed the tide of their declining fortunes. The doors of Arab prosperity opened up for Hyderabadi Muslims precisely when they had reached the deepest throes of frustration.

(2) *The Post-Police Action Plight* : As earlier stated that for the Muslims of Hyderabad, the period of late fifties, sixties and early seventies (which marked the beginning of prosperity in the Arab world) was the most gloomy one, in the post-Police Action era. The youth of this period was exceedingly frustrated as there prevailed massive unemployment even among educated young Muslims. Informants reported that many families were at their barest minimum with their bread winners earning through part-time jobs and private tuitions. Due to feudal traditions, there was a lack of spirit of enterprise, and therefore most of the young people could not become self-reliant. Among these frustrated youth, there were several young men who repentedtheir decisions to return to Hyderabad after the completion of their higher education abroad.

The plight of the lower middle and lower classes was the worst. A large majority of these comprised of those who had been pushed into the lower strata after the collapse of the feudal social order. The abolition of *jagirdari* system and the Custodian Property Act had reduced the feudal rich to utter poverty. Most of these individuals became jobless as they had no skills to be self-reliant, nor did they have any tradition or training for entrepreneurship. Rickshaw pulling became the monopoly of Muslims, and it was reported that some of the members of the elite class even took to begging, while some of the destitute women were forced into prostitution. Rural migrants from the neighbouring areas worsened the situation of Muslim poverty in urban Hyderabad. Many of these migrants simply became domestic servants or other menials and rendered service in return for just two meals a day.

Along with all these developments, Hyderabad and its environs were undergoing industrial expansion, but Muslims could not derive much benefit from it. According to our informants, discriminatory practices stood in the way. To this it may be added the Muslims on account of their long tradition of feudal life style had also not adopted themselves to the emerging industrial culture.

To summarize, the constant refrain of the informants was that even after two decades of Police Action, the condition of Muslims was generally one of penury. (Of course, in this study, it was not possible to establish the veracity or accuracy of such opinion.)

(3) *The Oil Boom : A Deliverance* : The oil boom of the Gulf countries, therefore, came as a deliverance and the opportunities were tapped through the Arabs of '*Barkas*'. Large numbers of Hyderabadi Muslims began to seek overseas employment. (Strictly speaking this movement to the Gulf countries may not be defined as migration in the sociological sense, since most job seekers are known to return to Hyderabad after passing a certain period of gainful employment.)

These job opportunities, and the consequent large inflow of money in Hyderabad has obviously affected Hyderabadi Muslims in several ways.

In the present chapter, an effort has been made to study the impact of petrodollars through detailed interviews with informants. This information was further supplemented by participant observation to the extent possible, and through the family histories of the 160 respondents.

Some preliminary observations that need mention here are that few job seekers are known to take their families with them to the Gulf countries. This was functional for saving money inasmuch as bachelor expatriates have few opportunities for socializing or entertainment in the Arab countries; also several expatriates share lodging and boarding and thus cut expenses. In some cases unskilled labourers are even provided with free food and shelter by their employers. Under these circumstances, most such expatriates are in a position to save a considerable amount and send back a large portion of their income. Upper middle class professionals, however, do take their families with them, but their high incomes generate considerable savings even after meeting living expenses. Thus in both cases Gulf employment has permitted a large section of Hyderabadi Muslims to be flushed with money.

(4) *Impact of Overseas Employment* : To reiterate what has already been suggested above, overseas employment changed the fortunes of the Muslim families in general, and of the middle and lower classes in particular. After years of deprivation, these families began to enjoy comforts and even own luxuries; furthermore a neo-rich class among Hyderabadi Muslims began to emerge. Affluence brought overnight responsibility in society and there emerged a new situation which was quite contrary to the one of the pre-Police Action feudal order, in which the have-nots were entirely at the mercy of the few haves. With the liquidation of the feudal order and this new opportunity for the lower and middle class families for acquiring wealth, a vast improvement in the standard and quality of life of the latter groups became possible. This development, however, has been a mixed blessing, inasmuch as the sudden change of fortunes has been too dazzling for individuals and families who had known life only as an ordeal.

One immediate impact of affluence among the lower and middle classes was a tendency to imitate the feudal elite's life style. For these classes the reference group had been the traditional nobles, *jagirdars* and the like, whose luxurious and extravagant ways were the ideals of these less fortunes; as human tendencies go, the deprived had always desired to emulate the aristocrats. Furthermore, the only value system which the Hyderabadi Muslims had known was the feudal value system, and in this system too an extravagant way of life was given top priority. Consequently, with the acquisition of Gulf money, the hitherto common people began to emulate their old masters in every way possible.

One visible manifestation of this has been the revival of traditional ceremonies. Even a common man is now in a position to perform the same celebrations which only the aristorcrats used to, say, some forty years ago. Conspicuous consumption has become the way of life with all sections of society. Individuals and families who for generations had a hand to mouth existence are now given to reckless expenditure and style of life. (A discussion on this is provided in the section on the rise of consumerism.)

But while the emulation of the traditional elites has occurred in certain respects, during her field work the researcher observed that etiquettes and sophisticate manners of the traditional aristocratic families had more or less died out. Aristocratic lifestyle and modes of behaviour do not easily develop among those who lack an elitist background.

With the breakdown of traditional feudal social structure there has been an obvious social change in a vertical movement of classes. The lower class emerged as a new middle class; the traditional middle class climb up on the social ladder and the upper class was simply crushed down of course with a few exceptions. This is evident in the tabular presentation below :

(5) *Utilization of Petrodollars* : Utilization of petrodollars, earned in the Gulf countries varies class to class.

As has already been discussed the economic crisis that followed Police Action had left all classes of Hyderabadi Muslims in a deprived state. But with the onset of the oil boom, overnight prosperity led to an economic revival with a strong accent on consumerism. The Muslims, specially in lower classes, just wanted to forget the hardships of the past to enjoy the present, without any planning for the future, just as they had done in feudal times. Informants provided the researcher with several examples of families which spent almost all their earnings in the craze of consumerism and saved nothing. But the researcher also found eases in which family members did realize the consequences of their extravagance and were worried about the future. They also feared to face their relatives abroad who were remitting funds to be saved and utilized in creating assets. But as they had suppressed their needs for a very long time - they could not resist the temptation to overspend now they had an opportunity.

The less irresponsible individuals/families do however utilize remittance to pay off old debts, and expenses incurred for obtaining visas to send family members overseas. After returning the loans whatever was left was reported to have been utilized for the purchase of real estate, gold, jewellery, repair of the old houses, securing back mortgaged property and in some instances, of buying life insurance policies. The researcher was also informed that the next priority item of unavoidable expenditure was to get their sisters and daughters married off to the worthiest possible groom, in terms of dowry and other expenditure. This statement was also confirmed in the course of researcher's interviews with her sample. Interviews with members of the Investment Guidance Bureau revealed that a cross-section of upper and middle class also invested funds in stocks and shares.

Providing opportunities for the children to acquire the best possible education is also considered to be a good investment, something for the parents to feel proud of. Accordingly, right from the very beginning of schooling, children are these days sent to best schools. Even lower class families are crazy about English medium education. So there is a demand for donations at the time of admission and young children have to go through difficult admission tests. After the admission, parents arrange for proper coaching at home. Tutors are handsomely paid. Much of all this has become possible because the head of the family is away in the Gulf region. In fact several house wives particularly in the middle class are staying in Hyderabad away from thir spouses just for the sake of their children's education so that they may personally supervise the monthly progress of their children.

Even in the lower class there is today an urge for English medium education. And one does come across instances of the children of domestic servants and rickshaw-pullers being sent to English medium schools. However, this is having a negative impact. As there is a lot of difference between the environment at home and in school, such children fail to adjust to the demands of the school and ultimately became drop-outs. It may be suggested here that these children, had they been admitted to Urdu medium schools, may possibly have completed their schooling.

When the schooling is completed parents, or rather mothers prefer to get their children admitted into professional or technical courses like medicine, engineering or computer courses etc. Parents are ready to pay exhorbitant capitation fees to some of the private colleges in the southern states. As regard daughters, bowing to the demands of the matrimonial market, parents crave for sets in medical colleges. The lower middle class which always have to rest contented with the second best in life opt for Unani medicine. The increasing demand for such courses has led to the opening of many private institutions which give admission on the basis of capitation fee. The amount varies from one lakh to five lakh rupees for medical degree course. For a degree course in engineering the capitation fee is forty to sixty thousand rupees, and for diploma course, twenty to twenty-five thousand. As compared to Andhra the neighbouring state of Karnataka has a number of colleges that grant admission on the basis of donations. Muslim families do not hesitate to pay huge admission amounts and bear subsequent educational and hostel expenses.

It may be mentioned here that in the perspective of the total Indian society some of these facts are not new or startling. However, when seen in the Muslim context, these developments are certainly noteworthy inasmuch as some twenty years ago no observer of the Muslim scene could have predicted that several Hyderabadi Muslims would reach such dizzy heights of affluence.

Those youth who do not get a chance to enter professional courses prefer computer courses or postgraduation and research in Geology, Genetics, Biochemistry, Microbiology, Pharmacy etc. There is heavy rush for admission in these courses also. The notable fact of change here is that Muslim students too are being drawn into science and technology courses which augurs well for the future of the community.

(6) *Changes in Religiosity*: The Muslims of Hyderabad as elsewhere had been God-fearing and believers in *kismat*. They had somehow carried an impression that the Muslim state of Hyderabad was beyond destruction, as if God Himself had promised for its security and safety. Even during Police Action, the informants reported, when the Indian army was entering from all the four sides of the state, Muslims in the

city could not imagine an experience so traumatic as the Police Action, until they were confronted with the victims who had fled from the rural borders to the city in search of refuge.

While the Indian troops were marching in, large sections of the population prayed for the victory of their forces. People expected that any moment some divine power would intervene on their behalf and help them out of their predicament. Muslim religious leaders went round strengthening the people's blind faith.

Even after the transfer of power and the Nizam's last address advising the people to be peaceful and cooperate with the new government, the local Muslims felt it to be a temporary phase.

It was only after some time that Hyderabadis realized that power had gone out of their hands forever and the change was permanent. Reflecting upon their misery they blamed themselves for the change. They came out with an explanation that God was unhappy with them because they had forgotten Him, and neglecting the principles of Islam had given importance to the luxuries of material life. There was a feeling of guilt and repentance, and a feeling that had they practised Islam in its true spirit they would not have faced such an adverse situation. It was generally because of such thinking that the Muslims became the victims of *aflas.* The introspection led to heightened religiosity in their lives, and one impact of this was that mosques became overcrowded.

The introspection also led to the desire to practise Islam in its pure form, and not to practise the customs and rituals that were un-Islamic. In order to preach and propagate pure or orthodox Islam, religious organizations like Tablighi-Jamat, Tameer-e-Millat and to a lesser extent Jamat-e-Islami, began to gain prominence; they emphasised what was in the *Quran* and *Hadith*.

The Tablighi-Jamat emphasized on spreading the principles of Islam especially among the rural and the urban poor.

Many educated Muslims from the middle classes played an active role in organizing camps within the city and surrounding rural areas. Prior to Police Action, as discussed in the Chapter on 'Traditional Hyderabadi Muslims Society', the religious functionaries were appointed by the government. Apart from these there were *Mashaikheen* or *Murshids* who monopolized this field. At that time there were no voluntary organisations to propagate Islam.

Another organisation responsible for arousing a new spirit of religiosity in the post Police Action period was the *Majlise Tameer-e-Millat*. There was growing influence of communist ideology among the Muslim youth of both elite as well as middle class background. It was a reaction of the new generation towards a decaying feudal social order where the lower classes felt deprived of their share in the prosperity of the state. *Majlise Tameer-e-Millat* played a very active role in diluting and even preventing the impact of communist ideology and atheism among Muslim graduates in particular, who were loosing faith in Islam and viewing its supremacy to be a myth; on the contrary, they were finding the radical ideas of communism more appealing. A lot of progressive literature was produced at that tims in Urdu prose and poetry. It was a time when to be a progressive meant being modern and intellectual. The common communists brought the Hindu and the Muslim youth together. Organisations like Tameer-e-Millat and Jamat-e-Islami in their efforts at arousing religiosity and preventing atheism only ended up in widening the gap that had been created between Hindus and Muslims.

(7) *Religious Enthusiasm—Rise of Fundamentalism and Witchcraft*: The chapter dealing with consumerism and cross materialism, earlier in this section, may possibly have led to the conclusion that along with these, secularization may also have increased. But this was not so. What happened to various communities in this country, as also to Muslims in other countries, materialism, interestingly, gave impetus to a rise in religiosity, fundamentalism, and communalism, on the other hand.

Thus, along with petrodollar affluence, Muslims in Hyderabad are tending increasingly to lean to religion. Prayers in the mosques are being attended by a larger number of people than ever before. A large number of voluntary associations devoted to religious activities have come into existence in the city. These receive substantial support through donations. As the local Muslims are well off, they are not averse to giving large donations for religious purposes. Large donations are particularly given for the maintenance of mosques. Some of the mosques today are decorated with very costly chandeliers and are fitted with decorative lights, fans and public-address systems for *Azaan*.

In the present period of religious enthusiasm more and more people are performing *Haj*. Several of these employed in the Arab countries now have funds to finance the *Haj* of their parents.

However it must be pointed out that along with heightened religiosity, there is also an increase in fundamentalism and the utilization (or misutilization) of religious scriptures for mundane and worldly purposes.

Our fieldwork revealed that there is an increasing evidence of orthodoxy among the lower classes and of orthopractcy among the middle classes. As regards magic and witchcraft, thouch strictly forbidden in Islam, have, surprisingly, found their way into Muslim families as well.

The masters of this "art" are called *Amels*, who are known to practise witchcraft. There is another category called the *Murshid*, which is becoming equally popular. The basic difference between an *Amel* and a *Murshid* was that the *Amel* was supposed to have control over evil spirits, whereas a *Murshid* is supposed to be a guide in matters concerning religious practices and the art of living. But the *Murshid* and *Amels* have become very much in demand among Hyderabadi Muslims, due to which many of them are earning even more than some qualified medical practitioners. They are invited in all family functions like Bismillah, Agiga, marriage and death anniversaries, etc. They are generally the "chief guests" on such occasions and are presented with costly imported items and cash. Some of the *Mureeds* of these *Murshids* bear the Haj expenses of these *Murshids*. Many persons have so much faith in the blessings of these *Murshids*, that they believe that by pleasing their *Murshids*, they can get various wishes fulfilled Many families believe that the blessings of these *Murshias* are responsible for obtaining employment in the Gulf and the subsequent prosperity of the family. Consequently, regular remittances are sent from the Gulf countries as gifts to the *Murshids* who were helpful.

Another important phenomenon that cannot go unnoticed is the visits to the *darghas* of the saints. "*Dargah-parasti*" (worship of *dargahs*) is also forbidden in Islam, yet practised by Muslims. Given the contemporary affiuence, many people are patronizing and lavishly spending on *urs*. *Qawuli* parties are organized and huge amounts spent on the maintenance of the *dargahs*.

Prosperity, it would seem, had also made people insecure and in order to overcome this insecurity they are resorting to witchcraft, faith in *Murshids*, *Amels* and *dargahs* and so on.

A healthy use of leisure time is a problem for the aged, particularly the males. These people are mostly found in restaurants. Gossiping in the restaurants, after breakfast for two to three hours is the daily routine. The researcher was informed that the range of discussions cover some current topics and some other topics of perennial interest to minority group members like conditions of the Muslims in India, affairs in Pakistan or Arab countries and America (as many of their friends and relatives are settled there), Iran-Iraq war, Palestine problem, communal riots in Hyderabad and in India and of course. last but not least, match-making is one of the most favourite pastime. Movies are not so popular among the males of this age group as compared to the females. Some of them, however, turn to religion and spend much of their time in mosques, and generally are very particular about offering *namaz* five times a day. Almost all these people whom the researcher contacted had either been to Mecca for *Haj* or were expected to go in the near future.

5

Muslim Class Structure

The Muslim feudal order : Interestingly, among the Hyderabadi Muslims, all Arabs did not enjoy the prestige and esteem given to them in other Muslim communities. In Hyderabad, except a few, majority of Arabs, because of their poor and backward condition, were considered "uncultured" and as a people who were to be helped financially, by virtue of their belonging to the land of Prophet Muhammed.

It was a tradition in Hyderabad to appoint Arabs on high posts in Police and Army since the period of Nizam III in 1803. But they did not enjoy any special status in the feudal society except that of the faithful employees of the Nizam.

In spite of all the restrictions which usually prevail in the feudal societies on social mobility, the tradition of conferring titles opened up the doors of inter-class mobility' inasmuch as individuals from various lower orders could seek entry into the "catch all" groups of '*Khan Bahadur*' and '*Jungs*'. To support the position that individuals from several occupation castes who migrated to Hyderabad from north India also managed to enter into these privileged groups in Hyderabad because of their outstanding services.

Historically, titles and honours were the legacies which the Nizams inherited from the Mughal Emperors. They adopted and perpetuated them as long as they were the rulers.

The hierarchical order of the honours was as follows:

(a) Titles of 'Jah' which were restricted to the royal family and nobles of the highest rank, for instance,
Asaf Jah—The dynastic title of the Nizam;
Khurshid Jah—Nobles of the highest rank;
Asman Jah—relatives of the rural; and the chiefs of the *paighah*
Arastu Jah—Prime Minister

(b) Titles bestowed on the higher nobility were :
Umara and Amir, such as:
Amir-i-Kabir, Amir-i-Azam Amirul-Umara, Shamsul-Umara

(c) The third category of titles, meant for the nobility of ranks below the above, were Mulk, Daula, such as Fakhr-ul Mulk Daula.

(d) Titles conferred primarily in recognition of services, such as Jung and Khan Bahadur.

Cash awards, grants of villages, *taluqa* or *Mahal* sometimes as *jagirs* for personal maintanace, sometimes in lieu of military service and occasionally for the purpose of farming.

Robes, comprising of pieces of unmade cloth, sometimes a long piece, often two or more were conferred on a person according to his rank and status. A *shawl*, turban or both also formed a part of the honour. The number of pieces indicated the rising degree of honour, such as *Khilat-i-yek parcha, seh parcha* and *haft parcha*. One significant point about these honours was thas they were graded to distinguish ranks according to the status of the nobles. Except in cases when the grant was made in perpetuity, the recipient alone was entitled to enjoy the honours and awards. (The chronology of Modern Hyderabad from 1720 to 1890 A.D., Hyderabad Central Records Office, Hyderabad Government, 1954, pp. v-viii).

Out of the four Sunni *Ashraf* groups, the Pathans of Hyderabad require a further clarification unlike the Saiyeds, Sheikhs and Mughals who are virtually like their counterparts in North India. The Pathans of Hyderabad are subdividied into the following categories :

(1) *Asli* or the 'real' Pathans—hailing from the North West Frontier Province of India.

(2) *Khitabi Pathans* or title holder Pathans—they are those who had served in the Nizam's army and were rewarded for their services with the title of 'Khan Bahadur', along with a huge plot of land as *jagir*. This group consisted of Sheikhs, Mughals, Pathans and a few Saiyeds also. But they were called *Khitabi* Pathans who used their title of Khan instead of their surname.

(3) *Kayam Khani Pathans*—They are the Rajput converts to Islam who served as reserve troops in the Nizam's army, and wére loaned to British government as and when it needed military help from the Nizam. They are more or less endogamous.

(4) *Mehdavi Pathans*—These Pathans form a separate sect as they believe that Saiyed Mohammed Jaunpuri was Imam Mehdi, whose birth has been forecast in the traditions (Holy Quran). This is an endogamous sect and does not marry among the other Pathans at all.

Having very briefly considered the four categories of Pathans characteristics of North Indian Muslims, it would now be relevant to compare and contrast these with the situation in Hyderabadi Muslims.

The three layers of the society i.e. the *Umra*, the *ausat tabqa* and the *ghurba* maintained their bounderies through in-group marriages. Thus even though the royalty gave its daughters in matrimony to the *paigah* family of nobility yet a social gulf remained (*paigahs* are explained later in this chapter). The informants repeatedly pointed out that each of the three group tended to marry within itself. Incidentally each group included Saiyeds, Sheikhs, Mughals and Pathans. The group boundaries were maintained through endogamy based largely on *firqa* (*Shia/Sunni*) and *tabqa* (class). Interestingly enough, even sect and class coincided but not the region (Deccani/Hindustani) the marriage will not be contracted among the middle classes. The regional differences were an important barrier not for *umera* but for the middle classes. Other things being equal cousin marriages among Hyderabadi Muslims were as popular as among North Indian Muslims.

But notwithstanding the general observance of endogamous restrictions exceptions have been reported by the informants. This is something totally against the North Indian tradition with a caste based feature the *Biradari* and the *Biahdari*.

The *Shias* some of whom also claim to be Saiyeds but are exclusively endogamous. Other endogamous groupings among the Muslims were the Navayatas, Bohra, Khoja, Mehdvis, Memons, Rohillas, Arabs, Labbe, Momins and Ladafs. These groups do not form an inherent part of Hyderabadi Muslims, except the Momins and Ladafs who were the neo-Muslims, or the recently converted lower caste Hindus. These stood by themselves neither did they marry outside their group, nor did anyone accept them in marriage.

As discussed later polygamy and concubinage was very common. Wives other than the first one or the keeps came from the families of lower classes. Most of them were Hindu converts from low castes. Their progeny constituted "second class" elites. They were never accepted in marriage by the nobility. A person with an inferior elite status of one family married another person of similar status.

As in North India, the Rajput converts to Islam known as *Kayam Khani Pathans* in Hyderabad continued to be endogamous; though included among Pathans, yet they did not enjoy an equal status. Their daughters were accepted in marriage by Saiyeds, Sheikhs, Mughals and Pathans but sons-in-law from the *Kayam Khanis* were rarely accepted.

In feudal Hyderabad there was a great concern for "purity of blood". For this reason there was great reluctance to contract marriage with non-Deccanis whether north Indians or Madrasis, in spite of similar rank and status, individuals belonging to these latter groups had been inducted in the Nizam's government. This concern of the Hyderabadis was something in contrast to what Mattison Mines has pointed out in his paper on 'Social Stratification among Muslims of Tamil Nadu (1975)'. According to Mines, the stratification among Muslims had nothing to do with purity of blood; instead concern for matching spouses was in terms of economic background and cultural and religious traditions.

In Hyderabad, there prevailed a condition parallel to what Siddiqui (1974 : 103) and Ahmed (1973 : 172) have investigated. Siddiqui has observed that among the Calcutta Muslims some sort of sanctity is attached to the purity of descent as is evident from the use of such terms as '*Sudh*' or pure against '*bisser*' or impure, *Najibut-Tarfain* as against '*birre*' or '*birrahe*' i.e. of mixed descent. Ahmed shows that in Allahabad the notion of ritual purity among the Sheikh Siddiquis is of such importance that it constitutes the main source of split between two marriage circles. He also points out that family geneology frequently used as a means of asserting this traditional purity of blood and bone, and that each family maintains a fairly detailed account of its descent and marriage as a proof of its purity of blood. In Hyderabad also, individuals both of whose parents were Saiyed were the most highly respected.

The religious functionaries (discussed in detail later in this chapter) are very much particular about the concept of *Najibut-Tarfain*. But the other groups were not so much concerned about this concept; they gave more importance to social status. The tradition of conferring titles was very much responsible in diluting the concept of ritual purity, if not totally eliminating it from society.

As discussed the existence of Muslim social groups in Hyderabad and the contrast of the Hyderabadi situation with the North Indian situation, we may now focus attention upon the pyramid of the social structure of pre-Police Action Hyderabad.

The Nizam and his family stood at the apex of the pyramid. If we trace back the ancestral history of the Nizam's we find that the founder of the dynasty Qamaruddin Khan, Nizamul Mulk was a commander-in-chief in the Mughal army and who was posted by Aurangzeb as the Subedar of Deccan. It is said that he was the direct descendent of the first Caliph—Hazrat Abu Baker Siddiq (Mudiraj, 1934).

After the Royal Family, the next group in the hierarchy was the *paigah*. The *paigah*s were a closed group of nobles of Nizam's period. The royal family had matrimonial relations only with the *Paigah* families and also gave their daughters in marriage to them. The word *paigah* is derived from Persian which means pomp and high rank. It was conferred as a title by Nawab Nizam Ali Khan Asaf Jah II upon his loyal military general Abdul Fateh Khan Tegh Jung Bahadur in acknowledgement and appreciation of the loyal services rendered to him. Ever since then the *paigah* family was honoured as a family of brave loyalists who were worthy of being allowed to take daughters of the royal family in marriage. The ancestral history of the *paigah* shows that Abdul Fateh Tegh Jung was the direct descendant of the Caliph Hazarat Umer Farooq (Mudiraj, 1934).

After the *paigah* nobles, ranked the *Umra-e-Uzzam*. These were the remaining families of the top nobles other than the *paigah*. This section of nobility consisted mostly of *Shias*, including the well-known family of Salar Jungs. Just as *paigah* was the family of skilled warriors, the *umra-e-uzzam* were considered to be able administrators. All these families had their origin in northern India, and had come to Hyderabad along with the First Nizam Qamaruddin Khan Nizam-ul-Mulk Asaf Jah I.

The next in rank were the feudal lords or *jagirdars* who had been allotted sizeable pieces of land, called *jagirs* for their achievements which mainly included military services rendered to the Nizam at the time of various wars. The first allotments of *jagirs* in the state were made by Asaf Jah I to his generals and those nobles and officials who acccompanied him from Delhi. These *jagirdars* not only enjoyed the right of revenue collection of the *jagirs* but were also responsible for its administration and were allowed to maintain independent civil and judicial courts. The system of allotment of *jagir* can be traced back to the times of Taimur, the lame, which was later adopted by Aurangzeb and was also followed by the Subedar of Deccan Qamaruddin Asaf Jah I. The *jagirdars* in return were allowed to maintain military contingents on the revenue derived from the *jagirs*, and were expected to render military aid whenever called upon for help.

Next came the *Magtedars*, who were awarded small pieces of lands but did not enjoy theright of administration. They were followed by *Mansabdars* who constituted the last rung of the nobility. For services that these families had rendered in the past, they were rewarded with cash pensions which were paid either on a yearly or monthly basis.

The above mentioned strata of nobility was followed by the salaried class, which constituted a large proportion of the Muslim population, employed in various administration posts in the government or in the offices of private *jagirdars*. Although these employees did not get very high salaries, they were largely contented groups because they identified themselves with the ruling class. They took pride in associating themselves with the implementation of laws if not with the legislation of these laws.

The feudal social structure, as in all feudal societies generated values inimical to trade and commercial activities. Not surprisingly, then, Hyderabadi Muslims whether, elites or otherwise, completely kept themselves away from the spheres of trade and commerce, considering these to be unrespectable means of earning livelihood. Consequently, commerce and trade, in the state of Hyderabad was controlled either by the Muslims of Bombay and Madras, or by non-Muslims. Muslim businessmen from Bombay included *Maimans*, *Bohras* and *Khojas*. Those from Madras, called *Labbe*, were involved in leather business. In course of time, some of the non-local Muslim businessmen were to attai n an all-India fame. One such prominent case is that of Vizir Sultan, whose enterprise became famous for Charminar Cigarettes. There were some others also. Local Muslims however lacked the entrepreneurship and thrift, and instead of investing money in productive channels, spent extravagantly in keeping up the feudal traditions of consumerism.

As is characteristic of feudal societies, notwithstanding the fact that the business community enjoyed greater affluence, it was the administrative salaried class that enjoyed higher social status.

The lowest strata in the Muslim social structure consisted of those who had no permanent source of income. There were generally illiterate masses without any skill and, therefore, totally dependent on the elites and the economically well-off sections of the upper middle classes. A majority of these poor were domestic servants, menials or beggars. The system perpetuated a feeling of dependence among the poor, who were content to lead a parasitical existence.

Poverty and dependence were also perpetuated by the institution of *Palakda*. The word *palakda* meant an adopted child. Usually these were poor children whose parents could not bear the cost of their upbringing. They were therefore left in the palaces and mansions of the elites and nobles who took over the entire responsibility of their upbringing. But since these children came from low socio-economic background, they lacked aspirations and could not utilize their opportunities, get educated and move up on the social ladder. Nevertheless, the adopted children were also given share from the property of the noble or the *jagirdar*, who had brought them up, and when the time for marriage came the *palakda* of one noble was married to a *palakda* of another noble.

The Muslim elites of Hyderabad had a tradition of maintaining huge troops of servants who were paid wages, but at the same time generation after generation, they were entirely dependent on their masters. They lived in the out-houses of palaces and mansions with their family members, and it was the responsibility of their employers to look after the entire family, and make arrangements including financial expenses for their marriages and even their children's marriages. Thus the patron-servant relationship had an in-built continuity in it and provided stability to this arrangement of mutual dependence.

Before the Police Action, beggars in Hyderabad were professionals, and were involved in begging for generations. Therefore, they were called *Khandani Faqeers*. Ironical as it may seem, these *Khandani Faqeers* took pride in begging and did not do anything else to seek release from their lowly position. They were supported by the nobles who gave them alms according to their status; much of the aims giving was linked to certain occasions, like festivals, etc. In this way, beggary and institutionalized charity were linked with each other, and encouraged the persistence of beggars and begging over generations. These above mentioned categories, namely, (1) beggars, (2) domestic servants, (3) *palakda* had institutionalized economic dependence among the lower classes. But the Police Action and the consequent collapse of the feudal social order gave this social parasitism a mortal blow. The *Jagirdari* Abolition Act of 1950 which reduced even rich nobles and *Jagirdars* to mere destitutes, who could no longer fulfil the responsibilities of their own families, drove the last nail in the coffin of these social parasites, and for several years after Police Action this strata of Hyderabadi Muslims were brought down to a very pitiable condition.

Many Urdu accounts give a clear picture of the Hyderabadi feudal social structure. One such account "Tazkera-e-Maashera-e-Hyderabad Deccan", by a famous Urdu writer Abu Zafar Moiduddin Hassan (1967 : 9-55), identifies the following main groups in order of their social status :

1. *Feudal lords*

   Umra and jagirdars
   Sahabzade, Murshadzade and Mansabdar

2. *Salaried Class*

   Government servants
   Employees of the jagirdars

3. *Religious group*

   Ulema Mashaekheen
   Qazi, Mohtesib, Khateeb, Narqi

4. *Professionals and Businessman*

   Lawyers, Unani and Allopathic doctors
   Architects and Contractors

A brief description of each group would be illuminating.

1. *Feudal lords* : This was the highest group of nobility ranked after the Royal Family. Apart from the nobles of the *paigah*, other prominent nobles included in this group were

Nawab Salar Jung, Nawab Fakhrul Mulk, Nawab Bahramud-daulah, Nawab Shaukat Jung, Khan Khanan, Nizamat Jung and many others. This class also included many Hindus. A few prominent ones were Maharaja Kishan Prashad, Raja Rai Rain, Raja Shiv Raj Bahadur and the Rajas of *Samastans* (Hindu mini states like the *Jagirs*), Vanparti, Gadwal, Gopal Peth, Jatpole, Rani Sarnapali, and many other *samastans*.

All the feudal lords of Hyderabad were absentee land-lords who were given the title of 'His Highness' and were entitled to gun salute. They were called *umra* plural of *Amir* meaning rich (Hassan, 1967).

Excepting the more prominent feudal lords like the ones mentioned above, many of them were illiterate and not well-versed in the art of administration. As all their attainments were secured on purely ascriptive grounds, they were totally unaware of the realities of life. With the exception of a few selected families most of the families had no tradition of higher education.

There were *Ayas*, *Annas* and governesses who were incharge of the upbringing of children of elite families. In addition, tutors were also engaged. In the late Asaf Jahi period, particularly that of Nizam the VI and VII, it had become a custom among the noble families to keep British and Anglo-Indian governesses and tutors to acquaint their children with western life style and etiquettes. As they did not undergo any formal education in schools and colleges, this training was a good substitute for them to be able to move in upper class society.

The feudal lords were generally polygamous and had a tradition of keeping a large number of concubines. The children born from these concubines constituted the "second class" nobility of the Muslim society. The children of the concubines of one noble were married to the children of concubines of another noble. While tracing the geneology, especially at the time of marriage, it was a common practice to consider only the paternal side of the person and not the maternal side. This practice was rationalized by such sayings as "*Tukhm dekho, zamin kyon dekhte ho*" ("see the seed and not the soil"). Such children enjoyed a limited share in their forebears' property, and were not entirely devoid of same respect; yet, they did not enjoy equality in the matter of property rights and social status with the legal children.

There was a troop of mistresses in the feudal *Harem* or *Deoris*, apart from lawful wives. The women of the *Deoris* (mansions) were divided into four categories—

1. *Shadi Ki Biwi* or wife-of-marriage : These were the wives who were formally married according to the Islamic law, as well as the local social customs. The marital negotiations were made by the family elders keeping in view the socio-economic status of both the famililies. Handsome dowry was an important feature of such marriages. The ceremony was performed by the state *Qazi* with traditional pomp and show.

The legal wife enjoyed the highest status among the women of the *Daori*. She was responsible for safeguarding the family customs and traditions. Around her revolved the entire life of the family. As she was incharge of the household expenditure she had a say in planning the family budget. Apart from her pocketmoney she was given special presents on the occasion of her birthday, and on the two *Ids*. She was not only honoured in her lifetime but even after her death. She was buried in the family graveyard in order of her position in the family.

2. *Manokha or the Nikahti Biwi* : She was next in the status of the wife-of-marriage. Though this wife was also married as per the *Nikah* laid dowa in the *shariat*, there was no popular approval of such a marriage. Such wives were generally taken from the lower classes and therefore they neither brought a substantial dowry nor were given a decent dowry. The noble or *jagirdar* husband only took the responsibility of her maintenance, and unlike the wife-of-marriage she was not entrusted with any of the family responsibilities. In most cases she did not even reside in ancestral palaces and mansions. But the children born out of such marriages were accepted in society and had an equal share in their father's property, like those of the children begotten by the wives of marriage.

3. *Khawas* : These were women who were never married to the nobles, and yet bore his children. The *khawas*

had the same status as mistresses or concubines. They were maintained in the *Daoris* by the nobles for purely sexual reasons. They lived in the out-houses of the mansions. On the occasions of the *Ids*, and the birthday of their masters, they were given some clothes and ornaments. The *khawas* who bore children were given special attention as compared to those who did not.

These concubines came from extremely poor classes among the Muslims, or from low caste Hindus, whose economic compulsions compelled them to enter into this relationship. But once they became *khawas*, these women were very instrumental in providing economic security to their parents' families. Thus, this was nevertheless functional for some poor families. Ironically enough, the down-trodden and indigent parents of the women took pride in calling themselves the "in-laws" of the concerned *Nawab* or *Jagirdar*. Verily, human beings seem to have an infinite capacity to adopt to oppression.

The easy wealth obtained by the feudal lords, and their over-indulgence in wine and women, kept them away from acquiring proper training in administration. As *jagirs* were ministates within the Nizam's kingdom, the feudal lords were entrusted with all the responsibilities of revenue, finance and the civil and criminal courts. But they were not fit to properly exercise the authority they had been entrusted. Consequently, the *jagirs*, and their subjects became victims of gross negligence. To compensate for their personal failures, the nobles used to rely heavily on their subordinates and, in fact, often became their puppets. The subordinates usurped power and exploited the innocent subjects. They became the real masters knowing well that the nobles had been reduced to nought.

Although the *jagirdar* class of Hyderabad state was characterised by all the evils of the feudal system, yet some of the great men of their times were born in this class. For example, great patriots, administrators, parliamentarians and statesmen like Salar Jung and Mukhtarul Mulk I, great poets like Mir Mehboob Ali Chan, Asaf Jah VI, Krishan Prashad and Moinudaullah, Nawab Nizam Yar Jung and Khan

Khanan, etc. were men who arose out of this decadent class. These nobles were great philanthropists, but their acts of charity made poor people their dependents and social parasites. They gave magnificent donations to the religious shrines at Mecca and Madina, and the *dargahs* of saints all over India and Hyderabad. They also contributed generously to various Hindu temples at Banaras, and other places including Hyderabad.

Mansabdars, Sahabzadas and Murshadzadas

(i) *Mansabdars* : The tradition of *mansabdars* can be traced back to the Mughal period, *Mansab* was a fixed amount of money given as a reward for the achievements of the individual or those of his ancestors. *Mansabdars* were responsible for maintaining the armed forces for the ruler. After the subsidiary alliance with the British, there was no need for the Nizam to maintain huge armies, yet the *mansabdars* continued to get their *mansabs*. Many *jagirdars* were given *mansabs* in addition to their *jagir*. To begain with, the entire *mansab* was inherited from father to son but later on only a small part of it was allowed to be passed on as inheritance.

(ii) *Sahabzadas and Murshadzadas* : *Sahabzadas* were the children of Royal *Khawas* who were related to the ruler on their paternal side, while the *murshadzadas* were children of the daughters of the Royal Family. Both the *sahabzadas* and *murshadzadas* were given pensions from the *sarf-e-khas* (privy purse of the Nizam) and they were also included among the *mansabdars*. Due to their claims on royal blood, both the *sahabzadas* and *murshadzadas* enjoyed a higher status than commoners. In order that others may identify them, *sahabzadas* used to put on a *Kalighi* (badge) on their turbans, and whenever they attended a *Darbar* or any other gathering all the *nawabs* and *jagirdars* irrespective of the size of their *jagir* or the amount of their *mansab* bowed before them. Abu Zafar Moiduddin Hassan (1967 : 35) has described an incident, to which he was an eye witeness, which illustrates the hierachical structure of Hyderabad's feudalism. Once when he was in the office of the then Prime Minister, Maharaja

Krishan Prashad, a person who was very shabbily dressed entered his office with a dirty badge on his turban. Krishan Prashad got up from his seat, bowed and welcomed him very courteously. The person was heard addressing the Prime Minister as "*Tum*", rather than the deferential "*aap*". Later on, it was discovered that he was a distant related *shahabzada* who had come in search of a job. The *sahabazada* and the *murshadzadas* treated all the government servants as their personal employees.

As this segment of nobility, the *mansabdars*, *sahabzadas* and *murshadzadas*, like *jagirdars* and other feudal lords, were free from the pressures of earning their livelihood, they spent a lot of time in leisure and merry-making. However, a few of them utilized their time and resources to patronize art, literature, collection of antiques and libraries along with their indulgence in hunting and other sports. Many of them constructed big and lavish palaces, summer houses and gardens. There are also some instances in this class, where young men went abroad for higher education and came to occupy high position of responsibility.

Salaried Class

This class came next to the *Umera* and was commonly known as *Ausat Tabqa*. In spite of the fact that financially they were weaker as compared to the businessmen or professionals (with the exception of lawyers) they enjoyed a much higher social status. As they were urbanites for generations they had no agricultural land. Though most of them own houses in the city, particularly in the old city.

Within these salaried class the more competent ones i.e. those who were matric or non-matric entered government service in various offices of the *Dewani*, *sarfe-khas* and other government departments like *malgozari* (Customs), (Revenue; *Abkari* (Excise), etc. as *Ahlekars* or clerks.

The remaining in this class who were less competent i.e. who were studied up to VII std. or those who had passed VII std. were absorbed in private *Jagir*. Excepting the more prominent feudal lords majority of these *Jagirdars* were illiterate and not well-versed in art of administration. It was these *Ahlekars* who actually looked after the *Jagirs* and managed them on behalf of the *Jagirdar*. Those in government were better paid as compared to those in private *Jagirs*. But irrespective of the fact as to where they were employed both were equally corrupt and accepted bribes in the name of Bali Amdani. They remained content with meagre salaries and these little bribes. They had no concept of saving or investment and lacked the spirit of entrepreneurship.

Instead they were the victims of false pride and in their attempt to emulate their masters they indulged in extravagance. Most of the time they were indebted to the Marwadis. The main occasions for taking these loans were none other than Aqiqa, Bismillah engagement or marriage of the daughter. They felt that they were under the social compulsion to celebrate them to the extent possible on the same scale as their masters.

Majority of Muslims of pre-Police Action days were in this class and it was a matter of social prestige for them to be in this class. They enjoyed the satisfaction of being a part and parcel in running the government.

It was really interesting to see the informants recalling the image of a typical *ahlekar* dressed in *Sherwani* and *roomi topi* (faz cap) with a *toshedan* (tiffon carrier) on the bicycle. It was the condition of the bicycle that spoke of the cadre of the clerk.

The only aspiration which they struggled for throughout the life was to make their children matriculates or at the most graduates so that they could start their carrier as second grade clerks. It was considered shameful for them if any of their children entered business. There was absolutcly no chance of upward mobility except that one got the title of Khan Bahadur for their outstanding performance in or one became a lawyer. Most of the doctors of pre-Police Action period all came from this class. As it was a profession held in low esteem the nobility would not let its children take up this profession.

This class kept away from wine and women business fact. Polygamy and concubinage so prevalent among the elites was considered absolutely improper in this class. Majority in this class were monogamous partly because of economic reasons and partly because of middle class morality. Though they had a large number of children and other dependents and meagre means of earnings yet they had a harmonious and peaceful family life.

Religious Functionaries

These included the following: (i) *Mashaekheen* and *Amel* (ii) *Qazi, Mohtasib, Khateeb* and *Narrui.*

(i) *Mashaekheen and Amel*: This was a highly charismatic group in the Hyerabadi society. *Amel* were involved in the practice of witchcraft and hypnotism, but on the basis of religious scriptures. *Mashaekheen* came into existence to guide Muslims in matters concerning religion. But in course of time, for mercenary reasons, they deserted this social responsibility and involved themselves in practices forbidden by Islam. The gullible masses came to believe that these people had evil spirits under their control and could help their followers out of any crisis. Their followers were called *mureed.* The *mureed* respectfully called the *Mashaekheen murshad.* The basic difference between the *amel* and *murshad* was that the *amel* was supposed to have control over evil spirits, whereas the *murshad* was supposed to be a guide in matters concerning religious practice and the art of living.

The *murshads* and *amels* were influential among the women folk, who approached them for common problems like ill-treatment by the husband or in-laws, barrenness or the marriage of daughters. They asked the *murshad* to pray for them and give *Taveez.*

(ii) *Qazi, Mahtasib, Khateeb and Narqui*: In the early Asaf Jahi period the *Qazis* worked as the judge and settled the disputes; but later on in the period of the last Nizam they were called only at the time of marriage to solemnize the *nikah* and the granting of the marriage certificate.

Mahtasibs were responsible for stopping people from committing like drinking, gambling etc. They were also responsible for the maintenance of religious shrines of Hindus, Muslims, Jains, Parsis and Sikhs etc. The state recruited them.

Khateebs were responsible for the oration of *Khutba* at the time of *Ramzan, Id* and *Bakrid.*

All these three positions existed in the government office for religious matters called the office of *Umoor-e-Mazhabi.* This department was abolished after Hyderabad was merged into the Indian Union.

(iii) *Professionals and Businessmen*: Both these were included into a category called *Azad Pesha,* meaning those who were self-reliant or with an independent profession.

Both professionals and businessmen, irrespective of their wealth and earnings, were placed below the nobility. This was so because in the feudal order they were required to toil hard and be competitive enough to earn their living. In the feudal value system, work, if it was for the purpose making a living, even if it required training and skills, was looked down upon. Professionals were regarded as the hired servants of the nobility.

(a) *Lawyers*: Like other professionals, laywers too were not respected. Till 1918, when the Law College of Osmania University was established, there was no formal degree college for studying law. Those from the elite families who could afford to study abroad and took a degree in law did not feel it worth practising as a profession. So for a very long period this profession was monopolized either by the Muslims who came from the North, or Hindu castes like Ayyangars and Iyers from Madras, or the local Naidus.

(b) *Hakeems and Ayurveds*: In spite of the fact that Unani medicine was very popular until allopathic system of medicine was introduced, yet, the *hakeems* like other professionals did not enjoy a very high status. Most of the *hakeems* came from north India. The Nizam tried to modernize the *unani* medicine to the extent possible. He started a *unani* hospital—*Shafakhana* along modern lines, like an allopathic hospital. But as allopathy became popular among the elites, the masses also started preferring allopathic treatment. The establishment of the Osmania General Hospital by the Nizam completely turned the people from *unani* medicine to allopathy.

(c) *Allopathic Doctors*: For quite some time, doctors as

professionals did not command much respect. People even refused to give them their daughters in marriages as there was prejudice against the medical profession. "No one is going to marry his daughter to a person who is involved in disgraceful acts of examining people's stools and urine" was the general prejudice. Due to the stigma attached to the medical profession, Muslims of Hyderabad did not enter it, and the profession was monopolized by Europeans, and Hindus. The Muslim doctors such as there were came from Madras and Poona, and other cities.

A medical college was established with Urdu as medium of instruction, which was later replaced by English. After police Action, when Muslims were discriminated against in employment, the medical profession gradually became acceptable as it assured an independent means of learning livelihood. In present day Muslim society of Hyderabad, doctors are enjoying the highest prestige, and are entitled to maximum dowry in marriage.

(d) *Merchants and Traders*: In spite of being an economically affluent group, merchants and traders were ranked very low in the pyramid of Muslim social structure. Hence Muslims, particularly in Hyderabad city, generally avoided taking upto business and shopkeeping, excepting trade in beaf, and selling of bangles and *mithai*. Such Muslim traders were rural migrants who had settled in Hyderabad, who still had links with their native villages and therefore had a value system different from these socialized in the feudal set-up.

(iv) *Menials and Domestic Servants* : Due to the existence of feudal economy, there existed a full-fledged institution of domestic servants among all the well-to-do classes of feudal Hyderabad. This institution was more prevalent among the upper middle class professionals and the salaried class of Muslims among the institution of *palakda* was not so common.

Depending upon the duties assigned to them and the responsibilities entrusted, there existed the following categories of domestic servants:

(a) *Anna*: She was the highest paid maid servant and was responsible for breast feeding and nursing infants. Usually these women were from poor but respectable families. It was a common practice among the rich to keep *annas* for their children. An *anna* of a Muslim family was always a Muslim. They were rewarded with small pieces of lands as *Maqtas* (orchards and vineyards) for their services, and were treated with considerable affection and respect.

(b) *Aaya*: This was next important maid-servant of the family. She looked after the children. It was not necessary for her to be a Muslim; there were Hindu and Christian *aayas* also. Among the *jagirdars* the *aayas* were kept to assist European governesses. But among the middle classes they assisted the mother.

(c) *Mama*: This female was the family cook entrusted with all the responsibilities of the kitchen. Usually she used to be a Muslim.

(d) *Mughlani*: She was also a Muslim female well versed in the art of tailoring. She was responsible for stitching and repairing the clothes of the whole family particularly that of the ladies, as it was considered indecent to get ladies' clothes stitched by male tailors.

(e) *Kamatan*: This maid servant was a low caste Hindu responsible for all the washing and cleaning of the house. Even those sections of middle classes and the salaried class who could not afford any other servant had at least a *Kamatan* to assist the housewife.

(f) *Mali and Malan*: Usually they were a couple employed for looking after the huge lawns and gardens around the palaces and *Daoris*. They belonged to a low Hindu caste.

(g) *Chhokri*: This used to be a young maid-servant most inexperienced of all and was not assigned any particular duty. She was to assist all the servants as and when needed. She could be from any community.

(h) *Syce*: He was employed for looking after the horses in the backyard of *Deoris*. Not only the feudal lords but even the upper middle classes maintained their own conveyance which were horse driven carriages. At one time, the *Syces* were in great demand. But later on when motor cars came in vogue and could be afforded by the *Jagirdars*, the *Syces* were employed only by the upper middle class who could not afford automobiles.

(i) *Mashalchi*: Last of all came the *mashalchi* who was responsible for the lighting arrangements of the large *Daoris* since there was no electricity. Adequate lighting arrangements were made by a number of lamps and the chandeliers around them constituted important pieces of decoration. Cleaning and oiling them was the responsibility of the *Mashalchi*.

(j) *Bhoi*: He was employed for all sorts of tough household jobs which the female servants could not do. This included grinding spices, carrying heavy things from one place to another and cleaning big utensils.

By way of summary and conclusion of this section, it may be said that as in all Muslim feudal societies, in Hyderabad also the ideal egalitarian society emphasized by Islam was not found. Though like U.P. the Muslims of Hyderabad were not divided into *Ashrafs* and *Ajlaf* but more or less similar restrictions were imposed on interaction and marriage between the three *tabqa*—the *Umera, Ausat Tabqa* and *Ghurba*.

There was a social gulf between the *strata* or *Tabqa*. The group boundaries were maintained through endogamy based largely on *firqa* (*Shia/Sunni*) and *Tabqa* (Class). Individuals had their position in society according to their family background. There were equal chances of finding *Saiyids, Sheikhs, Mughals*, and *Pathans* in all the three strata.

The surname 'Khan' among Hyderabadis was a bit more confusing. It was also a title given to *Saiyids, Sheikhs, Mughals*, apart from being the surname of *Pathans*. Business community in Hyderabad included non-Hyderabadis as the feudal values of Hyderabad held business in low esteem.

Social Mobility

As was the case with all the feudal societies, the social position of various groups and individuals in the traditional society of Hyderabad was quite rigid and almost immobile. In terms of social values, too, in feudal Hyderabad, the desire for upward mobility and achievement were not significant concerns. Hence such modern and highly esteemed professions like doctors, engineers, etc. were held in low esteem by the feudal elites, and it was only individuals who were outside the circle of elites who aspired to enter these professions. Of course, even when such individuals had achieved professional status they were not considered to be a part of elite.

Traditionally education particularly, among the elites, was not acquired for any instrumental reasons. During her survey the researcher came across many old people (now in their eighties) who had foreign degrees in Law but did not ever think of practising Law. As they were absentee landlords they could afford a luxurious life without practising the profession for which they had been trained. Another important reason for this delinking of education and jobs was the feudal value that it was improper to utilize one's knowledge and education for earning a living. As has been pointed out earlier the contempt for professional education was such that people were reluctant even to accept a doctor as a son-in-law.

To what extent has this situation changed? The data collected on this dimension has been presanted in Table 1. Obviously, the phenomenon of mobility has a class character inasmuch as different classes respond differentially to the opportunities of mobility as and when these open up. Consequently, the comprehensive data presented in Table I (see appendix) has, for purposes of convenience, been summarized in Table 1 to reflect the situation in three classes of respondents, namely, upper class, middle class and lower class. We begin first with the findings concerning the upper class situation as in Table 1.

Respondents from upper class families: Table 1 shows that out of the 30 upper class respondents who were studied, 30 had achieved upward mobility inasmuch as they came from families that were ranked as middle class in the feudal society. Of the remaining 20 cases, there has been no change in status. The individuals concerned had an upper class family background and had stayed there.

Respondents from middle class families: Turning now to middle class respondents, it first needs to be recognized that in the feudal order various middle class occupations like *tahsildars*, police inspectors, etc. were characterized by considerable nepotism. One got into these positions by virtue

Table 1

(Summarized form of Table I) Family Background and Mobility Pattern of Respondents

Family back-ground of respondents	*Upper class*	*Middle class*	*Lower class (Skiled)*	*Lower class (Unskilled)*
Upper	20	—	2	8
Middle	30	50	4	—
Lower (Sk)	—	—	24	—
Lower (Unsk)	—	—	—	22

of kinship and other similar connections. Consequently, it was not unusual to find generations of given families being confined to such occupations. As in all feudal societies, in Hyderabad too all business and commercial activities were held in low esteem. As such, Muslims who were not in elite groups preferred being in middle class ranked occupations with meagre salaries, rather than entering business.

In Table 1 we find that all 50 cases of our middle class respondents had a middle class family background. Therefore we can say here that middle class shows a picture of no change among Muslims as there is no case of upward downward mobility.

Combining now the upward mobility pattern of 100 respondents (50 upper class and 50 middle class) it is seen that 30 out of 80 respondents with a middle class family background, managed to move upward while the remaining 50 continued to stay on the same socio-economic level as their parents were. A point worth stressing here is that most middle class respondents had managed to save themselves from a downward movement in spite of the fact that there had been a liquidation of Muslim nepotism after the Police Action.

Respondents from the lower class families: The data on family background of 60 lower class (skilled and unskilled) respondents reveal that while the vast majority, i.e. 46 out of 60 cases had the similar family background, interestingly, 10 cases out of 60 were from families who once were feudal elites. This example of downward mobility illustrates as to how some of the elite families were adversely affected by the changes following Police Action. Exact detail of such decline is seen in Table 1, which shows that 2 respondents from ex-elites became cauffeurs and 5 took up rickshaw pulling, 2 became domestic servants, 1 who was the worst victim even became a beggar, and lost his mental balance due to sudden loss of ancestral property. Remaining 4 had middle class background.

There has been both upward as well as downward mobility; also, in the middle class respondents there has beea generally a no change situation.

The fact that needs recognition here is that in spite of the reversal of fortunes caused by the Police Action, there does not appear to have occurred a very large scale and drastic decline in the status of upper class and middle class Muslims, though as has just been seen, cases of downward mobility were present.

Here it may perhaps be worth making a comparison between the situation of north Indian Muslims and Hyderabadi Muslims. In former case, as scholars of Indian Muslims have repeatedly pointed out, very large sections of north Indian middle class Muslims migrated to Pakistan creating a vacuum in the socio-economic and socio-political life of the Muslim community left behind. This did not happen in Hyderabad, where notwithstanding the onslaught of the Police Action, the Muslim middle class was neither wiped off nor reduced to poverty. Since sufficient numbers of educated middle class Muslims remained behind in Hyderabad, when the next phase of change, namely, migrations to west, became available Hyderabadi Muslims were able to take advantage of the new opportunities that were materially beneficial to them. Hyderabad, unlike north India, had a large reservoir of educated middle class Muslims. For this reason, the frustration and alienation among Muslims here is less in evidence than in north India, where it is largely individuals and groups belonging to lower class background who are competing for mobility.

As rcgards these upper class Musli ns who suffered downward mobility, it may be observed that these were individuals who had been careless with the wealth they had possessed during their days of prosperity. Neither did they equip themselves with education nor any other training. Similarly their dependents' family (including their large army servants) had no skill or occupation of their own it was due to this that some individuals with this background became the worst victims of the socio-political changes following Police Action. In the course of interviews these once rich but now poor respondents indicated their once aristocratic background. As may well be imagined such individuals are finding their role reversal to be quite traumatic. They are experiencing the agony of "have-nots" while living with the memories of a world in which they belonged to the community of haves.

Another important point regarding the agony of lower classes is that had they possessed any occupational skills and not remained idle dependents of the feudal aristocrats or not been satisfied with simple domestic service of feudal families, their economic position today would have been much stronger as that of many of the artisan groups in north India.

At this point it may be worth making another contrast between the state of north India Muslims and Hyderabadi Muslims. This comparison or contrast is with regard to the educated middle classes. Contrary to the large scale exodus of educated urban middle class Muslims to Pakistan from north India, Hyderabadi Muslims generally stayed behind in India. The storm of Police Action shook them but did not whip them off, nor their education allowed them to descend into poverty. Hence unlike in north India, the Muslim community here was not left with a vacuum in the middle class and when the second phase of social change, namely, migrations to west began, large numbers of middle class educated Hyderabadi Muslims were available to cease the new opportunities. These brought stability in their lives and unlike in north India where individuals and groups largely from lower class backgrounds are now seeking to enter middle class position and difficult competitive conditions, middle class Muslims in Hyderabad are less prone to frustration and alienation so characteristic of north Indian Muslims.

Family background of the wives of the respondents: The upward mobility of individuals, particularly in open societies is often linked with finding a wife from a family that is advantageously placed and can bring benefits to the male partner. There is therefore greater frequency of males making marriage alliance with families above their rank and position than vice-versa. In feudal societies where status is relatively frozen such marriages were less frequent because status consciousness was so strong that families did not wish to be stigmatized for having stooped low in order to find appropriate sons-in-law. But as the erstwhile feudal society became more open and considerations of status consciousness began to defreeze, marriage alliance in which one could jump over one's own rank or position and seek alliance with family of superior status in order to attain upward mobility became more common. To match this tendency among ambitious and talented young men, parents of marrigeable daughters, in non-feudal societies, are willingto overlook the traditional considerations of family background and give greater emphasis to eligibility in terms of education, occupation/professional and income of potential sons-in-law.

Under this sub-heading an attempt has been made to examine whether the above stated general sociological truism is valid for Hyderabadi Muslims also. In Table II (see appendix) and in summarized Table 2 family background of the wives of the respondents is presented, depending on the profession/occupation of the wives' parents, their family background is divided into upper, middle and lower classes, and against this data, the data on the respondents' present status has been cross-classified in order to see the extent to which change has occurred in the norm of isogamy.

Family background of the wives of the respondents from upper class: Therefore out of the 50 cases of upper class background, 20 took their wives from the same class. Of the remaining 30 upper class respondents, 10 respondents acquired upper class status and notwithstanding their original middle class

Table 2
(Summarized form of Table II)
Family Backgrour.d of Respondents' Wives

Family background of wives	*Upper class*	*Middle class*	*Lower class (Sk)*	*Lower class (Unsk)*
Upper class	30	—	—	—
Middle class	18	50	—	—
Lower class (Sk)	—	—	24	7
Lower class (Unsk)	2	—	6	23

family background by marrying the upper class girls. These individuals were accepted as sons-in-law by the upper class families because of their outstanding educational qualifications and potential for success. It seems professionals particularly doctors were an exception to this consideration. None of them was accepted by the upper class as sons-in-law. So 7 of them married among middle class Muslims and three married non-Muslims (1 middle class Hindu Kayastha and 2 lower class Christians).

The point that needs stressing here is that in the feudal society this kind of social mobility would not have been possible for youngmen with middle class background. At the same time, however, it must also be recognized that a majority of a present upper class respondents who were originally from middle class families, did not achieve mobility through marriage but because of their own education. Also, it is interesting that all of the 20 respondents with upper class background married within their own social class. Both these facts go to show that while some change has occurred, yet it has not been very drastic and at least in the matters of marriage alliance, it would be seen that marriage within one's own kind of family background continued to remain widely prevalent even after Police Action.

Family background of wives of respondents from middle class: Out of 50 respondents in the middle class none married in the upper or lower classes. They all took their wives from the same class. This is supportive of the generally strong tendency in the middle class to observe isogamy. Thus, just as we observe a sort of stagnation, immobility and the change in occupational structure of this class, we also find a restriction on their matrimonial alliances. This is indicative of the fact that in the middle class perhaps the mobility due to change in occupational structure and one's opportunities for matrimonial alliance seem to be interlinked.

Family background of wives of respondents from lower class: All the 60 (skilled and unskilled) lower class respondents obtained spouses from families of their own socio-economic background.

An important point worth mentioning here is that 10 of our lower class respondents, who originally had an upper class family background, were compelled to seek their wives from the lower class due to their socio-economic status after Police Action (Tables I and II).

Change in Educational Attainments

As has been seen already, high educational attainments, particularly in professional education were never a very strong value among the feudal elites. Their status did not depend upon education; furthermore, in the feudal value system those who could enjoy the aristocratic life-style without having to work for it were respected and admired. The few who did get attracted towards education, did not seek it for instrumental reasons but rather for sharpening their other accomplishments. As acquisition of education was, on the whole, of low priority in the feudal value system.

In feudal Hyderabad, with the establishment of Osmania University some change did occur and various strata of people were drawn towards education. But these generally were those that were outside the circle of feudal aristocracy. For the non-elites, Police Action had drastically overhauled the feudal set-up; besides, some other developments also impressed upon Hyderabadi Muslims, particularly of upper and middle classes, that their future lay in education.

Table 3

(Summarized form of Tables III and IV)

Level of Education of the Respondents and their Wives

Level of Education	*Upper class*		*Middle class*		*Lower class (Sk)*		*Lower class (Unsk)*	
	R	*W*	*R*	*W*	*R*	*W*	*R*	*W*
Illiterate	—	—	—	—	9	16	20	22
Can read Quran	—	—	—	—	1	10	6	3
Can read and write Urdu	—	—	—	1	8	4	2	—
Education upto V std.	—	—	—	2	3	—	2	—
Education upto VIII std.	—	—	—	12	3	—	—	—
Non-Matric	—	—	—	10	4	—	—	—
Matric	—	—	6	3	2	—	—	—
Basic trained	—	—	3	9	—	—	—	—
Intermediate	—	27	14	3	—	—	—	—

Engg. Diploma	—	—	4	—	—	—	—	—
Graduates	4	9	8	4	—	—	—	—
B.Ed.	—	5	3	5	—	—	—	—
M.B.B.S.	—	6	—	—	—	—	—	—
B.E.	19	—	6	—	—	—	—	—
LL.B.	—	—	6	—	—	—	—	—
Postgraduates	10	3	6	1	—	—	—	—
Ph.D.	6	—	—	—	—	—	—	—
Specialized professionals	12	—	—	—	—	—	—	—

In the present micro analysis, an effort has been made to assess the extent to which there has been a change in the educational attainments of the families of the respondents in three generations. The data obtained for the three classes has been presented in Table III (see appendix) and in summarized form in Table 3.

Education of respondents from upper class: In the parental generation of 30 present upper class respondents, who had a middle class background, none had a graduate father. Of that remaining 20 respondents (who had an upper class family background), 2 fathers were postgraduates, 4 were Law graduates.

Considering now the level of education of the upper class respondents themselves, it may be said to be excellent. Most of them had even higher qualifications than required for their jobs.

Out of 50 respondents in this class, 6 in the legal profession, 7 doctors, 6 engineers and 8 university teachers had been abroad for higher education.

Professional education played an important role in assigning the present upper class status to most of the respondents. And perhaps this was the first generation of technical professionals among the Muslims of Hyderabad (see Tables I and 1).

Education of respondents' mothers and wives from upper class: Majority of the 50 respondents' mothers were illiterates, except 13 mothers who could read Quranic scriptures and 8 who could read and write Urdu. Women of this generation were not educated beyond this level.

When we consider women of the following generation, to which respondents' wives belong, change had occurred in educational levels of the women.

In this class of the sample the minimum level of education was intermediate and was attained by 27 wives out of 50. Out of the remaining 23, 9 were graduates, 5 had B.Ed. degree 6 were doctors, 3 were postgraduates (Table 3).

Education of respondents' children from upper class: The total number of children in 50 respondent families of this class is 182, with the age being below 30 years. All these children had acquired good professional and higher education. They had entered these courses through competitive examinations and successfully established their merit. This was true of both male and female children.

This generation of upper class Muslims had come from families with professional parents, who had encouraged them to seek professional education. A reinforcing reason for this was preference for an independent career, so that they do not remain dependent on government or private service in which they may have to face discrimination.

Out of the total of 182 children, 71 per cent were doctors and engineers. The number of females in higher education was very impressive, though they were much less in engineering but almost double their male counterparts in postgraduate courses. Two children of University were doing Ph.D. Very few children opted for Law (which was traditionally a prized profession) came from families of lawyers (Table 4).

Those children who were in natural sciences, social sciences and humanities did not stop at graduate level but went up to postgraduation. The number of such degree holders was highest among the children of university teachers.

According to the figures from Table 4 it is seen that out of a total of 182 children in the upper class, 2 daughters had B.Ed. degrees, 47 sons and 37 daughters had M.B.B.S. degrees, 38 sons and 4 daughters had B.E. degrees, 4 sons and 2 daughters had LL.B. degrees, 16 sons and 30 daughters were postgraduates and 2 sons were registered for Ph.D.

As regards education of children in western countries, it was informed by the respondents that out of a total of 107 male children, 38 went to western countries for higher studies, out of 38 only 7 returned back to Hyderabad. U.S.A. has been the most favourite country for settling down and those that did have eventually called their other brothers and sisters. For the latter particularly, the American green card has been a help in marriage.

Education of respondents from middle class : Not a single respondent in this class had a matriculate father, though

Table 4

(Summarized form of Table V)

Education of Children in Upper Class Families

Upper Class	*Male*	*Female*	*Total*
Illiterate	—	—	—
Can read Quran	—	—	—
Can read and write Urdu	—	—	—
Educated upto V std	—	—	—
Edcated upto VII std	—	—	—
Non-Matric	—	—	—
Matric	—	—	—
Basic trained	—	—	—
Intermediate	—	—	—
Graduate	—	—	—
B.Ed.	—	2	2
M.B.B.S.	47	37	84
B.E.	38	4	42
LL.B.	4	2	6
Postgraduate	16	30	46
Ph.D.	2	—	2
Total	107	75	182

these fathers had been in service. Obviously, their level of education had been very poor, but in those days it was possible to get jobs on the basis of family contacts and other connections. So the level of education was unimportant and even marginal education was adequate. This is what we found. Out of 50 fathers, 8 were non-matric, 12 had studied upto VIIth std., 20 upto Vth std. and 10 upto IVth std.

Now, coming to the generation of respondents while all of them were in similar kind of white collar jobs as their athers had been, their education attainments were much better. Times had changed and this was the first generation of Muslims after Police Action that came out in the job market.

Table 5

(Summarized form of Table V)

Education of Children in Middle Class Families

Middle Class	*Male*	*Female*	*Total*
Illiterate	—	—	—
Can read Quran	—	—	—
Can read and write Urdu	—	—	—
Educated upto V std.	—	—	—
Educated upto VII std.	—	—	—
Non-Matric	—	—	—
Matric	—	—	—
Basic trained	—	—	—
Intermediate	—	12	12
Graduate	35	35	70
B. Ed.	8	21	29
M.B.B.S.	29	26	55
B.E.	20	—	20
LL.B.	—	—	—
Postgraduate	8	14	22
Ph.D.	—	—	—
Total	100	108	208

Therefore the educational qualifications required for particular jobs had become essential. Also, the motivation to compete and survive in the new setup became important. Middle class Hyderabadi Muslims of those days tried to meet the requirements of changing times. Thus we see that out of 50 respondents not a single one was below mátriculation level and a few even had postgraduate qualifications in this class. This fact is revealed in Tables III and 3. The highest number (14) were educated upto intermediate level and there were 8 graduates. The respondents of this group also had professional and technical qualifications. Six of them had B.E. degrees (which they obtained after entering service), 4 had earned diploma in engineering, three respondents had B.Ed. degrees and there were 2 basic trained teachers. Some of the respondents had completed their additional qualifications through evening colleges, which goes on to show the desire to respond to the needs and challenges of time.

Education of the respondents mothers and wives from middle class : Out of 50 mothers of the respondents, only 7 could read and write Urdu and 12 could read Quranic scriptures and remaining 31 were illiterates. In those days it was not at all essential to educate women.

Regarding the level of the respondents' wives Table 3 shows that out of 50 wives in this class, only 1 had a postgraduate degree. The maximum number (12) had been educated upto VIIIth std., 3 of them were even below this level. There were 10 who studied till matric without passing it, another 3 had passed matric, 3 were intermediates and 4 had completed graduation. Professional education was also found in this class. There were 9 basic trained teachers and 5 had B.Ed. degrees.

Education of respondents, children from middle class : The total number of children in the middle class families that were surveyed was 208 out of which there are 100 males and 108 females. Table 5 which deals with educational level of children reveals that out of 100 male children 29 were M.B.B.S. and 20 had B.E. degrees. There were 8 with B.Ed. degrees. Out of remaining 37, there were 8 postgraduate degree holders and none below the graduate level. Education of daughters was also widespread in this group. The professional education was emphasized here also. There were 26

M.B.B.S. doctors and 21 had B.Ed. degrees. Of the remaining 61 children, 14 were postgraduates and 35 had studied till graduation level. The lowest level achieved was intermediate with there being 12 daughters in this category.

Out of a total of 100 male children, 14 sons went abroad for higher studies and settled down there. In this case too, the sons who had in U.S.A. facilitated of their other brothers and sisters.

Education of respondents from lower class (skilled) : Out of 30 respondents in this group, 8 were drivers : out of which 6 had illiterate fathers and 2 who came from feudal aristocratic families had matriculate fathers and the remaining 22 families knew just how to read and write.

Now coming to the generation of respondents out of a total of 30 respondents, 9 were illiterates, 1 could read Quran, 8 could read and write Urdu, 3 were educated upto V std, 3 upto VIII std, 4 studied upto X std but could not get through in the examination and 2 were matriculate.

Education of respondents' mothers and wives from lower class (skilled) : All thirty mothers of respondents were illiterates except 2 who could read Quran. Out of 30 wives 16 were illiterates, 10 could read Quran, 4 could read and write Urdu.

Education of respondents children from lower class (skilled) : As Table 6 shows that out of a total 174 children in this group 45 (29 males and 16 females) were illiterates. 53 (31 males and 22 females) could read and write Urdu. 35 (20 males and 15 females) were educated upto V std. 14 (4 males and 10 females) were educated upto VIII. 15 (10 males and 5 females were educated upto X but could not pass the exam., 4 (3 males and 1 female) were matriculates. All the four were basic trained and 4 (2 males and 2 females) were intermediate.

Education of respondents from lower class (unskilled): Out of 30 respondents, 8 who had come from feudal aristocratic families, 2 had matriculate and 6 had graduate fathers. But the remaining 22 had illiterate fathers.

Now coming to the respondents' education, 20 out of 30 were illiterates. Out of other 10: 6 could read Quran, 2 could

Table 6

(Summarized form of Table V)

Education of Children in Lower Class Families

Level of Education	Male	Female	Total	Male	Female	Total
	Skilled			Unskilled		
Illiterate	29	16	05	59	65	124
Can read Quran				14	14	28
Can read and write Urdu	31	22	53	7	6	13
Educated upto V std.	20	15	35	10	2	12
Educated upto VIII	4	10	14	—	—	—
Non-Matric	10	5	15	—	—	—
Matric	3	1	4	3	2	5
Basic trained	—	4	4	—	—	—
Intermediate	2	2	4	—	—	—
Total	99	75	174	93	89	182

read and write Urdu, and 2 were educated upto V std. (Tables III and 3)

Education of respondents' mothers and wives from lower class (unskilled): Out of 30 respondents, 8 coming from feudal aristocratic background had literate mothers who could just read Quranic scriptures. In the generation of wives, 3 could read Quran and rest were illiterates (Tables IV and 3).

Education of respondents' children from lower class (unskilled): Out of a total of 182 children, 124 (59 males and 65 females) were illiterates, 28 (14 males and 14 females) could read Quran, 13 (7 males and 6 females) could read and write Urdu, 12 (10 males and 2 females) were educated upto V std., 5 (3 males and 2 females) were matriculates.

The overall picture of education in the lower class that emerges from this sample is not very encouraging. Majority of the lower class continued to be deprived of education. Those 10 respondents in the lower class (2 in skilled and 8 in unskilled) who had come from feudal aristocratic families, in spite of the fact that they had graduate and matriculate fathers and literate mothers they themselves could just read Quran and Urdu. As perhaps this was the main reason for them to be included in the lower class after the abolition of *jagirs*.

Another important point is that the *Madrasas* in the mosques that teach the reading of Quranic scriptures and impart religious education have played an important role spreading literacy particularly among the lower class.

Professionalization of Respondents' Wives and Children

Females in the age group of 50 years from the upper class families who had been socialized along traditional lines, were never keen about taking up a profession in spite of their being educated. Several of them had ancestral property or other means, and their husbands were on highly paid positions and, therefore, there was no need for them to supplement family income. This further encouraged them to stay at home. The few who were in the professions from this class were mainly there for personal satisfaction.

But in the same cohort in the middle class families the attitude towards accepting a job was different. As family means were not adequate there was need to supplement. As can be seen from Tables IV and 3 on female education, though a majority of women from this class did not have higher education, yet they took up some suitable jobs just to augment their family income.

In the lower class of the same generation there was no question of professions, the women were either wage earners or were engaged in petty shopkeeping like flowers, *paan*, vegetable and fish selling, and so on.

As Table 7 indicates in the upper class families, out of a sample of 50,32 were housewives, 7 were school teachers,

2 were inspectresses of schools, 3 were university teachers and 6 were medical doctors.

In the middle class out of 50 wives, 20 were housewives, 6 were clerks, 8 were typists, 14 school teachers, 1 bank employee and 1 university teacher.

In thc lower class (skilled) out of a sample of 30 wives, 15 were housewives, 8 were *aayas* and 7 were domestic servants.

Out of 30 respondents' wives in the lower class (unskilled) 3 were housewives, 10 were beggars, 5 were flower and vegetable vendors and 12 were domestic servants.

In the middle class the number of working women was more as compared to the upper class. This perhaps was due to the financial need which enhanced the adaptability to the new values. It shows that the middle class was coming with a zeal to fulfil the material aspirations, discarding the traditional values and taking due advantage of the broken chains of the feudal domination utilizing the new opportunities. In this class women accepted jobs as clerks, typists and bank employees where they were in contact with the mals members. apart from taking up school teaching.

Employment of women, particularly of those belonging to middle and lower class families received a push by the circumstances obtaining after Police Action. Since the financial condition of Muslim males was no longer stable and assured, many of the women began to step out of homes to augment family incomes. The favourite occupation was, of course, teaching. A large mushrooming of private schools, as well as of aided schools, opened up a large job market for women in the teaching profession, and there was a ready response from middle class Muslim women.

One cultural concession that further helped the employment of Muslim women was the practice of providing women employees in the offices and banks with separate corners where they did not run the risk of "male contacts". Female peons (*aayas*) were also appointed for their benefit. Gradually, this practice has come to an end. Data from Tables III, IV, 3, 4, 5, 6 on education of women and their employment reveals while women in upper class families had more educated women than the middle class, employment among the former was not popular and widespread due to the influence of the feudal traditions and also because of other means such as property and high salaries of their husbands. But in the middle class the situation was different. Whosoever was educated and got the opportunity to work, accepted employment because it was very essential for them to supplement their family income, which, as has already been pointed out, had become insecure and uncertain after Police Action.

As regards lower class women who had always been involved in menial occupations, disintegration of the feudal order was a very great setback. Ironically, the feudal times were also their hay-days. Besides their monthly salaries, they used to receive a lot of traditional "perks", which actually raised the value of their wages in real terms. Thus, on occasions like festivals, marriages, child births and so on, custom had fixed additional payments in kind and cash. All these came to an end after Police Action.

Data from Tables VI and 7 reveals that women from the lower class families made no improvement in their position and continued to remain low.

Professions of respondents' male childien: It can be seen from Table 8 that the second generation of Muslim youth in the post-Police Action period is to be found in the professions and other salaried jobs, in increasing numbers. Both middle and upper class it appears equally are successful in getting their children inducted into the professions.

Interview probes revealed that some of the children who could not qualify the entrance tests for professional courses, were sent to such medical, or engineering colleges that granted admission on the basis of donations. This heavy expenditure is incurred by parents who can afford it, because professional education is recognized to be the best investment. In this generation of respondents' children there was horizontal mobility in the upper class families, that is while there was a change in the nature of jobs yet it was a change within the elite professions only. As such, there was no real social mobility in either direction.

In the case of children of middle class respondents there was a marked change in the occupational structure, as a majority of them have entered into medical, engineering and university teaching professions. Very few of them have remained in jobs which have the same rank as their fathers.

Children of the lower class respondents did not show much change in occupational structure, very few have entered white collar jobs. A majority have remained on their parents' level.

Professions of respondhnts' female children: In this generation Muslim females were either in high ranking jobs—medical doctors, university teachers, etc. or at the most in the middle class job of teaching. They preferred being housewives rather than accepting jobs as clerks, typists, etc. unlike their mothers.

To begin with, it needs to be pointed out that the majority of employed women in this generation were found in the elite families or the lower class families. In the middle class females the percentage of housewives was higher than that of working women. Those daughters from the middle class who managed to enter professions like medicine and teaching (both at school and college levels) continued to be in service. Most of those working as typists and clerks resigned their jobs after marriage. But the daughters coming from the lower class continued to be in jobs as typists and clerks even after marriage.

In Table 9 those daughters have been counted as housewives who had no intention of doing a job, and those female children who the respondents reported were in search of a job and were doing nothing have been taking as unemployed.

In the families of upper class respondents, out of total number of 75 daughters, 17.3 per cent were unemployed. 64 per cent were medical doctors and university teachers. 10.6 per cent were school teachers. There were three exception 2 of them were working as engineers and 1 as lawyer.

In the middle class with a total of 108 daughters the percentage of unemployed females was higher than that of the upper class i.e. 28.7 per cent. 13.8 per cent of female children in the middle class were not interested in taking up a job and had become housewives after marriage. Highest percentage (32.4 per cent) of female children in this class accepted jobs similar to that of their fathers. 2 of the girls got employment in banks, 18.5 per cent of medical doctors and 4.6 per cent of university teachers coming from this class showed a remarkable intergenerational mobility and change in occupational structure.

In the families of lower class (skilled) respondents the percentage of unemployment was 16 per cent and there were 26.6 per cent housewives. From the remainder, 44 per cent were absorbed as domestic servants and *aayas* in schools and colleges, only a negligible percentage (7 per cent) has become school teachers. It gives evidence of some mobility.

The rate of unemployed daughters was lower in the lower class families than in the upper class families, but it was higher in the middle class families. The percentage of housewives was almost double than that of the middle class because the women were not qualified for respectable jobs and also there was no aspiration for a better standard of life. Lower class female children did not hesitate to accept any menial job.

Concluding the discussion on this table it can be said the children of upper and middle class could secure good jobs. There is about 20% unemployment in the middle class. In fact, the percentage of unemployment would have been still higher if there had been no opportunity of overseas employment. In the lower classes the position of the skilled was quite sound because they were self-employed and their condition improved further due to Gulf employment. But in the unskilled with the exception of one or two all of them had to accept menial jobs. The condition of the beggars was pathetic where majority of the children had taken up begging. In these lower class unskilled families it was the marriages of their daughters to the Arab Sheikhs which improved the financial condition of the family. This phenomena has been dealt with in detail in the Chapter on Overseas Employment and the Impact of Petrodollars.

Emergence of Neorich

Petrodollars have inevitably led to the emergence of a

Table 7

(Summarized form of Table VI)

Showing Profession of Respondents' Wives

Professional level	*Upper class*	*Middle class*	*Lower class (Sk)*	*Lower class (Unsk)*
Housewives	32	20	15	3
Inspectoress of schools	2			
Doctors	6			
University teachers	3	1		
School teachers	7	14		
Clerks		6		
Typists		8		
Bank employee		1		
Aayas in school/colleges			8	
Fruit vegetable vendors				5
Domestic servants			7	12
Begggars				10

neorich class among Hyderabadi Muslims. But interestingly this has led to tension and friction between the neorich and the traditional elites.

During field work it was observed that the old *deoris* of ex-*jagirdars*, many of which even today are in ruined condition are being purchased by the neoeich. On being interviewed owners of these mansions expressed their dismay on seeing the younger generation of the former low status *ghurba* in a purchase the ancestral property of the ex-elites. It was clear to the present researcher, that there were several injured egos, on this account, among the former *jagirdars* and the like. Indeed several of them reported that they would not have minded if Hindus of their own (respondents) status had bought their properties. But it was unbearable to see that those whom they had considered inferiors till yesteryears should now be occupying *deoris* with which glorious memories and

Table 8
(Summarized form of Table VII)
Showing Professions of Male Children of Respondents

Profession of Male Children	*Upper class*	*Middle class*	*Lower class (Sk)*	*Lower class (Unks)*
Unemployed		20		14
Beggars				8
Factory workers				27
Police contable				1
Shopkeeper			5	4
Postmen			1	5
Vegetable and fruit vendors				10
Motor mechanic				5
Peon			2	8
Domestic servant				3
Typist		9	2	
Clerk		12	2	
Driver			24	6
Tailor			25	
Welder			24	
Electrician			14	
School teacher				2
Doctor	47	7		
Engineer	38	19		
University teacher	3			
Civil servant	8			
Lawyer	4			
Bank employee	3			
Research scholar	4			
Total	107	100	99	93

Table 9
(Summarized from of Table VIII)
Showing Professions of Respondents' Children (Female)

Profession level (Female)	*Upper class*	*Middle class*	*Lower class (Sk)*	*Lower class (Unsk)*
Housewives		15	20	12
Unemployed	13	31	12	
Beggars				20
Factory workers				23
Vegetable and fruit vendors				1
Domestic servants			15	22
Aayas in school and college			18	11
Typists		10	3	
Clerks		10		
School teachers	8	15	7	
Doctors	36	20		
Engineers	2	5		
University teachers	12			
Bank employees	2	2		
Research scholars	1			
Lawyers	1			

nostalgia had been associated. This frustration was expressed in Amjad Hyderabadi's following couplet :

Kaise Kaise Ayse Vaise Hogaye
Ayse Vaise Kaise Kaise Hogaye.

Besides acquiring the properties of the ex-elite, the neorich Muslims were also in a position to buy buildings and other residential units, which after Police Action had passed from Muslim hands into Hindu possession. Several properties had been lost at the time of Police Action due to the Evacuee

Property Regulation. Some of these too have now reverted to Muslim ownership.

Besides the old city area the neorich have purchased plots of lands and constructed houses throughout the city. After Police Action the elite Muslim localities of Hyderabad like Banjara Hills, Khairtabad, Himayat Nagar, Hyderguda, Masab Tank, Kachiguda, Red Hills, etc. had predominantly become Hindu localities. With the inflow of Gulf money since 1970s onwards the situation had changed. Muslims have also started purchasing land in these areas. During this period, price of land had increased from hardly one rupee per square metre in 1950 to three hundred rupees per square metre in 1984. In a locality like Banjara Hills common Muslims could not purchase land, but now when the price of land in this locality has shot up to three hundred rupees they were in a position to bargain and buy. Quite a few of these are located near the Banjara Hills, an area which symbolizes the memories and traditions of Muslim aristocracy prior to Police Action.

The researcher came across a few cases, where ancestral property had been sold off due to poverty but given the savings from overseas employment, families and individuals were in a position to repurchase their old houses though of course at an enhanced rate. The researcher feels that estate building is one of the few gainful investments in which the Muslims of Hyderabad have invested their recent wealth. Several respondents revealed that they now owned or rented out the additional houses which has/have become sources of regular income. This changed situation, perhaps, brings a sense of satisfaction and well-being to the community.

Overseas Employment among the Respondents' Male Children

As emphasized earlier in the macrolevel discussion, since the oil boom Muslims of Hyderabad have secured jobs on a large scale in the Gulf which have served to strengthen the financial position of many Muslim families. Table 10 (summarized form) shows the position of overseas employment in the families that were surveyed in the present study.

Out of a total number of 399 male children from all the

Table 10

Overseas Employment among Respondents' Male Children

	Upper class	*Middle class*	*Lower class*	
			Skilled	*Unskilled*
Working in Gulf	75 70%	66 66%	82 82.8%	20 21%
Did not work in Gulf	32	34	17	73
Total	107	100	99	93

Total number of male children of all groups — 399
Total number of male children gone to Gulf from all groups — 243 (60%)

three classes 243 or about 60% took advantage of the available opportunities. The maximum advantage has been taken by lower class skilled families where it was found that about 82 per cent male children had gone overseas for employment. The upper and middle class families were behind with 70 per cent to 66 per cent children being employed in the Gulf, respectively.

In the upper class families the highest percentage of overseas employed was in the families of doctors (83.3 per cent). In the middle class families the highest percentage of incidence of overseas employment was among the children of school teachers (76.4 per cent) while in the lower class skilled families such employment was highest among tailors (88.8 per cent) followed by welders (84 per cent), electricians (80 per cent) and drivers (77 per cent). Even in the lower class unskilled families, it is seen that from among domestic servants and rickshaw-pullers as many as 31.5 per cent and 27.9 per cent families have managed to send at least one member of the family to the Gulf. However no such case was found in the families of the beggars, that were interviewed.

Quality of Life of the Respondents before and after Employment

Table 11 indicates a marked improvement in the quality of life of the respondents has taken place due to overseas employment. While the increased purchasing power due to petrodollars is the obvious cause for this it should not be forgotten that conspicuous consumption had traditionally been a strong value of Hyderabadi Muslims.

The homes of the families studied are today full of various gadgets. Interestingly, some of the lower class respondents admitted that they were possessing certain gadgets which they did not even know how to use since they were unable to follow instructions in English. Perhaps merely keeping them in homes served a prestige value.

In additon to gadgets, money has also been invested in gold ornaments and purchase and repair of houses. However, the respondents were not willing to disclose the exact weight of gold they had before and after overseas employment. Regarding the purchase of houses it was found that almost all of the respondents in the upper class and middle class had their own houses, consequent to employment abroad. Even among the lower class skilled families and lower class unskilled families about 83 per cent and 16 per cent, respectively had their own houses. The other household items they have are fans, bicylces and transistors, etc. (see Table 11).

Table 11

Quality of Life of the Respondents before and after Overseas Employment

Before Overseas Employment	*DH.*	*E.*	*C.*	*C.G.*	*Fan*	*Tr.R.*	*T.V.*	*S.*	*Co.*	*T.R.*	*F.*	*T.*	*VCR*	*Car*	*A.C.*	*Co.*
Upper Class (50)	48	50	—	40	50	50	40	23	10	50	30	38	—	21	2	18
Middle Class (50)	16	40	50	10	50	5C	15	10	—	35	5	—	—	4	—	4
Lower Class																
Skilled (30)	6	10	30	—	20	20	2	5	—	10	—	—	—	—	—	—
Unskilled (30)	—	—	8	—	10	3	—	—	—	—	—	—	—	—	—	—
	70	100	88	50	130	123	57	38	10	95	35	38	—	25	2	22
After Overseas Employment																
Upper Class (50)	50	50	—	50	50	50	50	40	40	50	50	42	39	38	10	43
Middle Class (50)	50	50	50	40	50	50	50	50	25	50	50	15	29	10	—	40

Lower Class																
Skilled (30)	25	30	30	25	30	30	30	30	20	30	10	20	10	5		10
Unskilled (30)	5	16	20	3	20	15	7	5	—	10	—	—	—	—	—	—
	130	146	100	118	150	145	137	125	85	140	110	77	78	53	10	93

N. B : D. H.=Own House ; E=Electricity ; C=Cycle ; C.G.=Cooking Gas ; Tr.R.=Transistor Radio ; T.V.=Television ; S.=Scooter ; Co.=Cooler ; T.R.=Tape recorder ; F.=Fridge ; T.=Telephone ; A.C.=Air condition ; Ca.=Camera.

6

Customs and Cultural Practices

Having examined the traditional social structure we may now turn towards a consideration of the traditional Muslim culture of Hyderabad—in order to more correctly appreciate the nature or character of the change that has occurred in the four decades with which we are here concerned.

The Muslim culture of Hyderabad referred to by the Hyderabadis as "Deccani" culture had an entity and uniqueness of its own, and was considerably distinct from north Indian Muslim culture. As a matter of fact, it was as unique as the well-known "Lucknawi" culture. Historically, it was a mixture of Indo-Islamic culture of Persian origin and the regional Hindu culture of Telangana, or more generally that of the Deccan plateau. Its roots can be traced back to Zafar Khan Allauddin Shah Bahmani, a Turk, who was initially appointed the Subedar of Deccan by Mohammad Bin-Tughlaq. Zafar Khan later on became the founder of the Bahmani dynasty in 1338 (Fida Ali, 1926). But it was the Qutub Shahi rulers of Golconda, particularly Ibrahim Qutub Shah and his son Mohammad Quli Qutub Shah, contemporary of Akbar, who nurtured Hyderabadi culture into a complete distinct cultural entity.

Ibrahim Qutub Shah, the father of Mohammad Quli Qutub Shah, was a great patron of learning and literature. He was a learned man himself and took keen interest in the diffusion of learning. He composed poetry in Telugu, Urdu and Persian. Some of the Telugu works produced during his period were dedicated to him because of the patronage he gave to Telugu poets and poetry. He was effectionately called Ibhram or 'Ibhramudu' in Telugu language (Makhdoom Mohiuddin, 1966). This impact of fusion of different languages brought about a cultural integration in the form of mutual exchange of words, expressions of art and literature costumes, food, habits, religious and social observances.

The son of Ibrahim Qutub Shah, Mohammad Quli Qutub Shah (1590-1612) the ruler and the founder of Hyderabad is said to be the first Urdu poet who published his collection of poetic work in the form of a *Diwan* (Hashmi, 1923). He was a Telugu poet who like his father patronized Telugu Urdu poets.

After 1724, when the Asaf Jahi period began it became the policy of Hyderabad's rulers to recruit competent men, if necessary, from outside Hyderabad in order to assure an efficient administration. Thus people from all over India, representing different culture and languages, were attracted to Hyderabad. As the Asaf Jahis themselves had been the prime inheritors of Mughal culture they followed the same tradition of appointing Muslims of Persian, Turkish and Arabic origin to constitute the highest officialdom. Among the Hindus, they brought with them, were Kayasthas from nothern India (U.P.), Khatris from Punjab and Braham-Shatriyas from Gujrat (Dharminder Prashad, 1982).

The ruler and the nobles patronized poets and literary men who developed Persian, Arabic and Urdu literature. Due to an enlightened policy of cross-fertilization of Hindu and Muslim culture, Hindu culture with preponderant influence of Telangana region influenced the Muslim culture of Deccani origin. This confluence of cultures that historically mingled together became a "Panchvani Sangam", and continued to prevail in Hyderabad State until the Police Action and subsequent modernization of Hyderabad's traditional society.

1. *The Daccani Calendar* : With the foregoing brief introduction, we may now describe some of the specific aspects of the Hyderabadi Muslim culture. A good starting point would be a consideration of the Daccani calendar, around which the major cultural events of local significance revolved.

It will be seen that while these events are in essence a part of the great tradition of Islam, yet in their actual observance there was a local colour and flavour peculiar to Hyderabad.

During the Nizam's regime, *Ilahi* and the *Fasli* calendar was adopted for official purposes, which had twelve months or 365 days in a year. The course of the year followed the apparent movement of the sun. It was therefore called *Shamsi* year. In 1335 *Fasli* (1946 A.D.) the government of Hyderabad amended the *Fasli* year by reducing the duration of the *Aban* month by five days so that the beginning of the *Fasli* year could coincide with the starting of the international calendar month, October (Dharminder Prashad, 1982).

The Fasli months with their English equivalents can be listed as follows :

Azur (October), Dai (November), Bahman (December), Isfandar (January)	Winter
Farwardi (February), Ardi Bashish (March), Khurdad (April), Teer (May)	Summer
Amardad (June), Shehrewar (July), Mehr (August), Aban (September).	Monsoon

For important events like Royal Proclamations, etc. both *Fasli* and *Hijri* dates were taken into consideration.

The *Hijri* months with their local equivalents can be listed as follows :

Hijri	*Local*
Muharram	Muharram
Safar	Teratezi
Rabi-ul-Awal	Maulood/Barawafat
Rabi-us-Sani	Gyarvin

Jamadiul-Awal	Madhar
Jamadi-us-sani	Hussain Shahwali
Rajab	Rajab
Shabaan	Shabaan
Ramzan	Ramzan
Shavval	Khali
Ziqad	Bandanvaz
Zilhaj	Bakraid

As listed above, almost all the *Hijri* months had their local equivalents depending upon their significance for the Hyderabadi Muslims.

Muharram, which had the same local name, became a month of special importance ever since it came under the *Shia* dynasty of the Qutub Shahis (1518 A.D.), the impact of which on the day to day life became inescapable and is to be seen even to this day. After the Qutub Shahis, the Asaf Jahis (*a Sunni* Dynasty) came to power but the *Shia* impact prevailed and was revived during the period of the last Nizam, Mir Osman Ali Khan, who was *Shia* both at heart and to a great extent in practice as well.

A detailed description of the observance of *Muharram* in the Hyderabad State can be conveniently divided into two phases : (1) under the Qutub Shahis (2) under the Asaf Jahis.

Muharram under the Qutub Shahi Kings

An Urdu account—'Daccani Culture' by Hashmi (1923) brings out the following details: since the Qutub Shahi dynasty was *Shia*, *Muharram* was observed with great reverence throughout the state and a sort of state mourning was observed. As soon as the *Muharram* moon was sighted music, singing and dancing were banned throughout the state, including the Royal Palace. Strict prohibitory orders were placed on selling and buying of all alcoholic drinks and meat. Chewing *paan* and smoking were also prohibited. All the citizens of the state wore black clothes. This continued till the 20th day of the month 'Teratezi'.

Majlises (religious meetings) were organized by the state to mourn the martyrdom of the Prophet's grandson, and his companions at Karbala. The happenings of Karbala were repeated every evening in the form of '*Marsia*' and '*Nauha*'. Every evening the king attired in black clothes himself used to attend these *majlises*. *Sharbat* (cold sweet drink) was served and food was supplied to all those who were present in the *majlis*. The Royal *aashoor khanas* were beautifully decorated with lights and colourful carpets. People of all religions, castes and sects would come to pay their homage. *Muharram* was popular among the Hindu subjects also, and was called by them as '*peera pandu*' (festival of the peers or saints) and Imam Hussan and Hussain were called Ashna-Ushna' in Telugu.

On the 10th of *Muharram*, which as the day of martyrdom of Imam Hussain, large crowds all clad in black clothes and bare footed, formed a huge procession, led by the king who was also bare-footed and attired in black clothes. This procession carried the *alums* to the river Musi, for immersion.

After the downfall of the Qutub Shahis the state of Hyderabad (or Golconda, as it was then called) came under the Mughals, who belonged to the *Sunni* sect. So *Muharram* no longer was a state sponsored affair and the Subedar of Deccan appointed by the Mughals did not attend it. The state did not finance the Muharram activities, and state sponsored mourning was not encouraged.

Muharram under the Asaf Jahis

In the early Asaf Jahi period a number of activities associated with the observance of Muharam were revived and generous grants were given by the government to the *aashoor khanas*. *Mujavars* were appointed by the state. But the king himself was not present in the *majlises*, as was the custom in the Qutub Shahi period.

As soon as the Muharram moon was sighted *alums* were installed in the *aashoor khanas*. The ruler himself used to carry a tray containing flowers to be offered to *alums* at various *ashoor khanas* along with *kichdi* (a dish of pulses and rice) and *sharbat* (cold drink) to be distributed among the poor and needy gathered there. Afther this the king returned to his palace. The playing of music at the royal palace, and at the mansions of the nobles and *jagirdars*, was stopped during the Muharram. Sad tunes were played at the *aashoor khanas*. *Alums* were installed in most of the places of the nobles and *jagirdars* irrespective of their sect—*Shia* or *Sunni*. People of all religions, castes and sects came to the *alums* and made floral offerings. This continued throughout the ten days of Muharram. Some people stopped eating *ghee* and salt during these ten days, while others remained bare-footed and observed fasts.

On the 10th of Muharram, the more popular *Alums*—*Hussaini-Alum*, *Bibi-Ka-Alum* and *Alum-Nal Sahab*—were taken out in processions to river Musi where they were immersed; the remains were brought back to their respective *aashoor khanas*.

This traditional observance of Muharram continued till 1911 when Nizam the VII Mir Osman Ali Khan ascended the throne. He prohibited unnecessary display and the taking out of processions, and the enactment of street corner plays depicting the life of Imam Hassan and Hussain. Instead, now solemn condolence meetings were held on large scale throughout the month till the 9th day of *Rabi-ul-Awal*. The *alums* were no more installed by the nobles and *jagirdars* who were not *Shias* All other processions were stopped except that of *Bibi-Ka-Alum*. Mir Osman Ali Khan was very much against the hypocrisy associated with the Muharram mourning.

An old social custom associated with Muharram which is still practised, by the more tradition bound, is that newly married couples are not allowed to stay together, and separated from the time of the sighting of the Muharram moon till the entire month is over (Hashmi, 1923).

Safar or Teratezi : *Safar*, the second month of Muslim calendar, was supposed to be the most ominous month and was locally known as *Teratezi*. It was a common belief that in this month countless evil spirits called *bala* were sent on earth by Allah. The only way to be protected from the malevolent influence of these spirits was to give *khairat*, alms, to the poor, throughout the month. On the full moon night of this month, oil, iron nails and eggs were kept by the bedside near the pillow of each member of the family. Next morning when they got up each of them was supposed to see his own shadow in the oil. This oil was then given to special beggars called '*Teli rajas*' literally, oil kings), along with the iron nails and eggs. Well-to-do families also sacrificed sheep, goats and cows and distributed the meat among the poor. For lunch, on this day, a special dish was prepared out of boiled grams. This was originally a Mughal tradition, which was later on followed in Hyderabad also.

The last Wednesday of *teratezi* which was known as *aakhri-chahar-shamba* was a day of special significance in the Deccani calendar. During the Nizam's rule it was observed as a government holiday. According to popullar belief, on this day Prophet Muhammad had come out for a walk for the last time after his recovery from the illness preceding his death. The celebrations on this day were marked by picnics and outings. Women who observed *purdah* also went for picnics with suitable arrangements for their seclusion. No marriages were performed in this month, and children born in this month were supposed to be ill-fated.

Rabi-ul-Awal : The twelfth day of this lunar month marks the birthday of Prophet Muhammad. This month was supposed to be very auspicious and was of equal importance for both *Shias* and *Sunnis*. The 11th and 12th days were observed as gazetted holidays during the Nizam's period. From the first of the month till the twelfth day, religious scholars spoke in public meetings about the teachings of Islam. Such gatherings were generally not attended by progressive people with western education. In the royal palace and the mansions of the nobles and *jagirdars*, banquets and dinners, which were open to both rich and poor, were held for all twelve days.

During the reign of Asaf Jah VII (1911-1948), on the night between 11th and 12th *Rabi-ul-Awal* the famous Mecca *Masjid* was specially illuminated and renowned religious scholars addressed public gatherings there. Such sermons were called *waaz*. It was a common practice to hold at least one such *waaz* in each locality and government office to mark to occasion of *Id-Miladun-Nabi*, which falls on the twelfth day of this month.

Some years later Bahadur Yar Jung, a social worker and a dynamic leader of Hyderabad, utilized this occasion for strengthening fundamentalism among the Muslim youth. Also during this period Osmania University organized debates on various aspects of Islam and other topics of religious importance. Even after Police Action, the *Id-Miladun-Nabi* function has continued to be organized regularly by several Muslim organizations such as *Tameer-e-Millat*, *Majlis-e-Ittehadul-Muslimeen*, etc. in which noted scholars from all over India are invited.

Rabi-us-sani : This month was also supposed to be one of the auspicious months, specially for marriages. Many *waaz* gatherings were organized. The most significant event of this month was *niaz* of Hazrat Ghaus-e-Azam Dastageer Peerana-e-Peer Abdul Qadir Jeelani, a renowned *Sufi* saint, popularly known as Ghaus Paak. Before Police Action the occasion of the *niaz* was observed as a government holiday. The details of the *niaz* are discussed in brief below :

This *niaz*, known *Gyarvinki-niaz* was performed on the eleventh day of the said month. Ghaus Paak was especially popular among business groups, both Muslim and Hindu. Indeed, his *niaz* was performed by the Hindus with great faith and devotion. *Biryani* (a non-vegetarian dish of meat and rice) was cooked and *Fatiha* (supplicatory prayer) was offered in the name of the saint, and the food was given to the poor and needy. Green flags bearing the name of the saint were put atop the houses. There was also a custom of making artificial graves by the roadside, in bazaars or other public places as replicas of his grave; green flags were put up on these pseudo-graves in his memory.

Rajab : This was considered to be the most auspicious month. Even otherwise, *Rajab* was full of celebrations and holidays; the 1st, 6th, 13th, 18th and 26th days were specially celebrated. The first day of the month marked the birthday of Nizam VII. On the sixth day the *urs* (death anniversary) of Khawaja Moinuddin Chishti of Ajmer, the famous *sufi* saint, was observed. Though the *urs* was actually held in

Ajmer, but Hyderabadi Muslims in large numbers offered *fatiha* in their homes. The 13th day of *Rajab* was celebrated as the birthday of the Hazrat Ali, the fourth Khalifa of Islam. As such, this day was of special significance for the *Shias*. On this occasion a procession popularly known as *Maula Ka-Sandal* was taken out on the seventeenth and eighteenth of this month. On the 22nd day of *Rajab*, the *niaz* of *Yasduham Shareef* popularly known *Koondon-ki-Niaz* was offered. The night of 26th *Rajab* was observed as "Shab-e-Meraj". On this night, according to the Holy Quran, Prophet Muhammad had visited Heaven.

All of the days mentioned above were observed as state holidays. A brief description of each celebration would be of relevance here.

The first of Rajab—Birthday of Mir Osman Ali Khan Asaf Jah VII

Being the Nizam's birthday the first of *Rajab* was observed as a holiday throughout the state and was celebrated with special gaiety in Hyderabad. Early in the morning, the Nizam went to offer special prayers at the Shahi mosque, at Public Gardens, from where he was escorted to *Fateh Maidan* (now called Lal Bahadur Stadium) to inspect a Guard of Honour. On this occasion the Arab regiment in the State's army had a special role. It prayed in Arabic for the health and long life of the Nizam. After that a twenty-one gun salute was presented. In the early years of his reign there was a lot of illumination of public and private buildings and dance and music sessions were organized all over the state. But eventually this celebration became a less gala affair. A special *darbar* was held on this occasion, which was attended by nobles and courtiers, *jagirdars* and *mansabdars* who presented golden coins called *asharfi*, to the Nizam. The number of *ashrafis* given were according to the status of each noble.

6th of Rajab—Urs Khawaja Ajmeri

The *sufi* saint, Khawaja Moinuddin Chishti of Ajmer, was very popular among the Muslims of Hyderabad. A large number of his followers went from Hyderabad to Ajmer to participate in his *urs*, which fell on the sixth day of *Rajab*. Special trains of the Nizam state railway were run on the occasion. Those who could not attend the *urs* at Ajmer sent their *nazrana* (money for floral offerings at the saint's grave) though those who went there, and offered *fatiha* at home in his name on specially cooked dishes; these were distributed among the poor, relatives and friends. Special *Qawali* programmes in the praise of the Khawaja were also organised on the occasion.

13th of Rajab—Birthday of Hazrat Ali

As is well-known, Hazrat Ali has a very special significance for *Shia* Muslims. As such, his birthday, which falls on the thirteenth day of *Rajab*, was observed on a grand scale by the *Shias* of Hyderabad. They celebrated it by organizing *majlis* (meetings to recall the brutal their relatives in the world). It was a common practice to visit the graves of relatives and offer flowers. This practice still continues. Delicious dishes are cooked and distributed among the poor in the name of their relatives, presumably for the peace of the departed souls. *Halwa* made from *suji* (cream of wheat) was specially cooked on this occasion. Mosques are beautifully decorated and illuminated. In addition, there was large scale bursting of crackers and letting off of fire-works. These are indulged in even today. It is believed that this celebration, which is found only among Indian Muslims, was popularized (killings of *Karbala*) at individual homes as also in various *aashoor khanas*. On the seventeenth and eighteenth of *Rajab*, *Shias* in large numbers visited the hillock of Maula Ali on the outskirts of Hyderabad in continuation of the birthday celebrations. This spot assumed the importance of a shrine during the Qutub Shahi period, because of the legendary footprint of Hazrat Ali impressed on a stone there.

22nd of Rajab—Koondon-ki-Niaz or Yasduham Shareef

This was the *niaz* celebrated in the honour of a renowned religious saint Imam Jafar Sadiq, who is buried in Baghdad. On this occasion, *kheer* (preparation of milk and rice) and *puris* (prepared from wheat flour and dry fruits) were prepared and kept in *koondas* and *fatiha* was offered. Many poor people were fed along with the invited guests. On this occasion, only vegetarian dishes were cookd. Non-vegetarian food was strictly prohibited.

Shabaan—and the Celebration of Shab-e-Barat

Shabaan is one of the sacred month of the Islamic calendar and was spent by the orthodox in meditation and prayers. The most important occasion of this month is the Holy night of *Shab-e-Barat*, between 14th and 15th of this month, when it is believed that the souls of the dead visited among the Muslims during the reign of Akbar, which marked the intermingling of Hindu and Muslim customs and traditions, etc. (Hashmi, 1923).

In Deccan illuminations and fire-works became a part of *Shab-e-Barat* celebrations in the period of Mohammed Quli Qutub Shah, a contemporary of Akbar and the pioneer of Deccani culture. It is from his poems that we learn that Hyderabad started celebrating this festival from his times with gaiety and enthusiasm. Dance and music sessions were also organized (Hashmi, 1923).

During the Asaf Jahi period, crackers and other fire-works were presented to the King by the *paigas*, the *Diwans* and the *jagirdars* as *nazrana*. In turn the King distributed the same to his nobles and courtiers according to their rank. All the employees of Nizam's government were given crackers as *Shab-e-Barat* gifts.

Ramzan: The month of *Ramzan*, as is well-known, has special significance for Muslims all over the world. As a Muslim state, Hyderabad naturally observed *Ramzan* with appropriate importance and sobriety. However, as in other matters, here too, Hyderabad had its own tradition of observing this month of fasting, penance and tradition.

In the Qutub Shahi period as soon as the *Ramzan* moon was sighted all the "wine-and-women" business and other activities of merry-making were prohibited throughout the state, including in the royal palace. Bars and wine shops all over the city were closed for the entire month. The King, along with all the members of the royal palace and its employees, observed the month-long fasts. In the population at large, nobody could be found publicly smoking or chewing *paan*, or consuming any other eatables.

During the Asaf Jahi period *taraveeh* (a special *namaz*) offered at night during the month of *Ramzan*) was offered in the mosques, in addition to the observance of the restrictions just mentioned. The mosques were decorated and illuminted during this month. *Iftar* (snacks taken at sun-set when the fast comes to an end) was sent to the mosques by the rich and well-to-do families for the consumption of the poor and needy. To begin with, only the nobles of the *paigah* and the *jagirdars* sent *iftar*, later on it became a common practice among all upper class elites; some people from the middle classes who could afford also followed this practice. On the last Friday of the month, which has a special importance for the Muslims all over the world, a special *iftar* was personally taken to the mosques by the *jagirdars* and the nobles.

At the end of the month, when *Id* was due, special arrangements were made to sight the moon, and as soon as it was sighted three cannons were fired to inform the people. (Actually this was a common practice on the sighting of each new moon).

Id-ul-Fitar was observed almost like a national festival. Government offices and all educational institutions were closed for a week. Special *Id* prayers were held on *Idgah* grounds which were also attended by the Nizam, along with other government officials. In a special oration (on the occasion of the *Id* prayers) called *Khutba*, people prayed for the health and long life of the King whom they called '*Zilullah*' meaning the shadow of God. After the *namaz*, twenty one cannons were fired as a salute to the King. All the government officers on their way back home visited the King *Kothi* (the royal palace) to offer the King their *Id* greetings and *nazrana* which consisted of *asharfis*. The number of *asharfis* depended upon the rank enjoyed by a particular officer. After paying respect to the King, the officials visited the houses of the nobles and *jagirdars* to offer *Id* greetings. Here they were served with *paan-supari* and *itar* (perfume); *sheer khurma*, a special sweet prepared for the occasion was also served. Even Hindu nobles observed customary formalities when their Muslim subordinates visited them on *Id* day. Raja Fateh Nawaz Jung, Raghunath Prashad, Raja Murli Manohar and Raja Inder Karan are still remembered for their hospitable acts at the time of *Id*. Maharaja Kishan Parshad (the than Prime Minister) used to hold a special *darbar* on this occasion which was attended by his subordinates. The Nizam himself organized a great *darbar* of *Id-ul Fitar* to confer titles on those nobles whom he wished to reward for their outstanding achievements. Those who attended this *darbar* had to be dressed in a formal *darbari* dress, which included *Dastar, Sherwani, Bagloos* along with the sword (Hashmi, 1923: 285).

Celebration of Id-uz-Zuha: Like *Id-ul-fitar*, the *Id-uz-Zuka* or *Bakraid* also was celebrated with great enthusiasm and gaiety. There was a five-day government holiday. The sacrificial animals were generally sheep. Very rarely cows or camels were also sacrificed on this occasion.

Customs Associated with Marriage: Ideally, Muslim marriage is a contract between man and woman settled on a certain amount of dower in the presence of a *Qazi*, and two male witnesses. All this is denoted by the simple ceremony of *nikah*. According to the Islamic law, *nikah* is the only requirement for a man and woman to become husband and wife. But after a long period of stay with Hindus, certain Hindu customs inevitably crept into the socio-cultural life of Indian Muslims. These non-Islamic influences were adopted with suitable alterations and modifications so that the essential Islamic requirements were not grossly violated. Some marriage customs which were Hindu in orgin and yet associated with Muslim marriages in Hyderābad were as follows:

Mangni: This is a Hindu custom meaning engagement. When the girl's and boy's parents reach an agreement regarding marriage this ceremony is performed. On this occasion the boy's parents and relatives visited the girl's house and presented some ornament to the bride. This was reciprocated by the bride's parents with a return visit. After the actual ceremony the bride's parents paid a handsome amount of money to the groom's parents. This was called *pindi*. It was derived from the Telugu word '*Pendli*' meaning marriage. This custom marked the beginning of marriage ceremony.

Manja: This was also a Hindu custom performed a few days before marriage. The bride was freed from all the responsibilities and duties in her parental family. After being given a ceremonial bath and dressed in yellow garments, she was made to sit on a yellow cot in an exclusive room in which all the furnishings were of yellow colour. *Manja* was observed for three, five, seven or eleven days, and every day a mixture of *Haldi* (turmeric), *chiksa* or *ubtan* (a herbal paste applied to improve complexion) was applied regularly by *suhagàns* (women whose husbands were alive).

Sanchak : One day prior to the wedding, the groom's party visited the bridge's place and bringing the wedding dress along with a few more dresses and jewellery. They also bring a lot of dry fruits, beetle leaves, beetle nut, catecheve, cloves, cardimum etc. The mother-in-law applies the ritualistic paste of *Haldi* and *chiksa* on the bride's face and *missi* (a black powder applied on lips) and decorate the bride with all the jewellery she had brought for her.

Mehndi: After *sanchak* the groom's party returns home. Now the bride's party visits the groom's place to perform the *Mehndi-ki-Rasam*. The bride's sister presents a ring to the groom and applies *Mehndi* (a greenish paste made from special kind of leaves, which gives a peculiar reddish tint wherever it is applied and then washed off after some time) on the little finger and the paste of *chiksa* and *haldi* on the face. For performing these services the sister-in-law was given *nek* (tip).

Dhingana: On the day of wedding as soon as the *barat* (marriage procession) arrives at the bride's place her brothers stop the procession and would not let the groom go in till he bribes them with a handsome amount of money. After that he is escorted to a decorated stage where the *nikah* ceremony is to be performed.

Nikah: The *nikah* was, and performed in the usual manner

followed by Muslims all over India. It is performed in the presence of a *Qazi* and two witnesses, the bride's father, brothers and a few other close relatives and friends and the groom signs the marriage contract. After this dry fruits, including almonds, dried dates and *misri* are showered up on the groom which are then taken away by the guests present there. The same thing is repeated in the *zenana*. But after the bride gives consent for the *nikah* certain local customs came into operation. For example, the groom's mother puts a *nath* (a big golden nose ring) in the nose of the bride and a necklace of black beads in round the bride's neck. These two ornaments are regarded as the symbols of married status and the bride is supposed to wear the necklace of black beads always as long as her husband is alive. The latter ornament was the same as the Hindu *mangalsutra* but it is called *Kali Pot Ka Lachha* among Muslims. After this the groom is brought into the *zenana* and made to sit in front of the bride. They both see each other in the mirror. This custom is called *jalwa*. The groom then presents a ring to the bride. After this, they both are garlanded and seen off for the groom's place.

Chauthi: On the day following the wedding, the bride's parents invited close friends and relatives for a dinner. It was more of an informal gathering and those present played with vegetables, and splashed water colours to celebrate the marriage.

Walima: The day after *chauthi*, the groom's parents invited the bride's party for a dinner. This was supposed to be *sunnat* (a practice of the Prophet of Islam). After dinner the couple were garlanded. With the *walima* the marriage ceremonies come to an end. Nowadays a new trend has came up and that is to have *Chauthi* together *Walima* on the next day of wedding.

Jumagi: Every Friday after marriage, the couple was invited for a dinner by the close relatives of the bride. This was called Jumagi. Four Jamagis were arranged by the bride's relatives. And the fifth, and the last one, was given by the groom's family. All the close relatives and intimate friends on both sides were invited.

The preceding description of rituals and ceremonies associated with various festivals and marriage will have indicated the extravagant life style of Hyderabadi Muslims. Besides this, there are a number of occasions connected with child birth and death when ceremonial functions take place, when huge amount of expenditure is done by the Muslims. This pattern of social life continued till Police Action. The nobles, aristocrats and other higher-ups in the society maintained the feudal tradition of lavish expenditure and extravagance on every occasion—big or small and satisfied their desire for social recognition by indulging in as tentatious celebration.

Dowry: In Arab societies, there exists the custom in which the bride's father received payment from the groom. But in India, under Hindu influence, the Hindu custom of dowry has been an unavoidable aspect of Muslim marriage.

Ideally, demanding dowry was considered to be wrong, yet, for pragmatic reasons no marital negotiation was complete without first setting dowry. Though the basis of initiating marital negotiation was geneology, family background and socio-economic status of both the families, yet among the non-feudal families considerations other than dowry were of secondary importance. While dowry was not openly demanded yet a tremendous lot was given by way of dowry.

In the middle classes, apart from the above mentioned considerations the groom's educational qualifications were also important. But tragically, his qualifications also determined his bargaining strength, in the matrimonial market. The higher the qualifications, the higher was the dowry he could demand and get, though the matter was settled in very discreet and indirect way. (Possibly, while the institution of dowry has been widely prevalent among Muslims there has been a sort of a guilt feeling over it, since it is not an Islamic custom). In the lower classes the prime consideration was whether the man would be able to provide his family two square meals a day or not. Depending upon this the issue of dowry was bargained by both the parties.

In the present chapter traditional Hyderabadi culture has dealt in detail the emergence of new synthetic cultural entity nurtured under the Qutub Shahi and Asaf Jahi dynasties, Deccani calendar, the details of festivals and celebrations of local importance, customs of marriage and the life style of the feudal age. It has vividly depicted the socio-cultural conditions prevailing in Hyderabad at the time of initiation of change.

7

Muslim Life-style, Family and Status of Women

Life Style

It would be worthwhile to briefly consider the daily routine of the aristocrats and elites to show how the daily life of the elites reflected their affluence.

As the *jagirdars* and *mansabdars* were free from the worries of daily existence, they spent their time in leisure and merry-making and hardly had time for any serious work. Their daily routine began at about nine or ten o'clock in the morning with a lavish breakfast of *khichdi*, *khatta*, *papad-badian*, *paratha*, *keema*, *kabab* and other delicacies. After this, the rest of the time was spent in gossip, cockfights, gootfights, chess, gambling and other such games. Lunch would be around three in the afternoon and included lavish *Deccani* and Mughali dishes like *baghare baigan*, *korma*, *dam-ki-marghi*, *biryani*, etc. From evening till midnight there were sessions of music and dance. In these sessions, and at other times as well they freely imbibed imported liquor, in addition to a country liquor called *sendi*. Most of these individuals were also addicted to opium.

This indulgent and comfort loving life had made these people unfit for anything. They were completely dependent on servants, who used to carry water to the toilets and waited there to wash the master's hands when toilet was over. Even for performing *wazu* (washing of hands and face before each *namaz*), they needed a servant.

Obviously, this easy way of life was not characteristic of those belonging to service class businessmen, and the skilled and unskilled labourers. They had to begin their daily routine early morning and put in a lot of hard work to maintain themselves. Differences, however, did exist (as they do in all societies) between the middle and lower classes. Thus according to the middle class it was considered shameful to indulge in gambling, drinking and keeping concubines. Hence they kept away from these vices, but the lower classes were habituated to all these. Among the latter both men and women were addicted to *sendi.*

It is interesting, however, that while in their practices, the middle class did not emulate the easy-going feudals, yet, in terms of aspirations they desired somebody to be in a position in which they could enjoy in the manner in which the elites did. These latent aspirations were revealed on occasions of marriages, and other similar events, when the extravagance of the lords and nobles set the norms and standards for emulation by those lower down.

In brief overall structure and the associated value system of Muslim society in Hyderabad remained basically feudal, until it was given a crushing blow by the Police Action. However, as will be seen later on, Hyderabadi Muslims did not completely forget their cultural traditions in spite of the profound changes that affected their society after 1948. In recent years as the Gulf boom and some other favourable economic factors have restored, to some extent at least, affluence among many Hyderabadi Muslim families, evidence of a return to some of the traditional extravagant ways has been available. It seems that there has, overall in these four decades, existed a latent desire to return to the glorious of Hyderabadi culture of feudal times.

Traditional Muslim Family and Status of Women

Our discussion of the traditional Muslim social structure and culture of Hyderabad cannot be complete without a brief exposition to the status of Muslim women and the Muslim family of Hyderabad.

Regarding women, Elizabeth Cooper (1915) observed that the Muslim women of the feudal period were very much dependent on her husband. However aristocratic the family background, women were not at all educated. They were kept totally ignorant about the world beyond their *deori* doors, though they were not compelled to wear *burqa*. Very strict arrangements were made for their segregation. Husbands were very much reluctant in allowing their wives to make new acquaintances. Indeed, it was the husband who decided whom his wife shall visit. He made sure that the house to be visited was well secluded and the hostess had no "advanced" ideas, and also that the husband of the women to be visited was a man of good reputation. All this concern on the part of the husband was regarded as a desire for protection, rather than deprivation of liberty.

As regards the daily routine of the women of elite families, Cooper has very well brought out their slow and easy going life in which "my lady" woke up at eight in the morning and got ready for breakfast, with the assistance of innumerable maids, after full two hours. Breakfast would be followed by visits of friends, relatives and other "hangers-on". Since there were virtually no domestic responsibilities, afternoon would be devoted to silk merchants and jewellers who would send their wares right into the *zenana* through their female representatives. These shop-women not only did business, but were also great gossipers and would communicate all the news from other *zenanas*. Purchasing was done after a great deal of bargaining, which went on till the late hours of the evening. In the night, the husband or sons would visit the women's quarters and bring the Begum the news of the world outside. Thereafter came dinner time, and retirement for the night.

Interviews with informants confirmed this leisurely routine of these upper class Muslim women. All the responsibilities of the household including child rearing, were entrusted to the house-keepers, governesses and an army of servants.

Thus, the women of the upper class families led uneventful and purposeless lives. They neither served themselves, nor were of any use to others.

Of course, women in middle class and lower class

families were not so fortunate, and had to struggle through life.

In the traditional Muslim society of Hyderabad dowry was supposed to be the female's right on her parents who in turn felt privileged to give as much as they could to their daughters. This in turn won her a lot of respect and regard from her in-laws when she joined them. In spite of all this she had a subdued status in the new family until she herself became a mother-in-law. As the family was patriarchal, the sons brought their wives to their father's home. The feudal homes were large and sheltered many families. The mother was the head of the women's chamber and her word was law. Innumerable servants and poor relatives were ever present for her assistance.

Though there was no intellectual compatibility between the husband and wife because of their differential exposures to the outside world, yet women had full control on their chamabers and had their say in home management. By and large, women's spheres of authority and competence were entirely different from those of males due to which there was mutual dependence and recognition for each other's contribution. But this division of labour did not confer any advantage to women. Secluded behind *purdah* and without any other economic security except their husband's support, they were totally dependent on them and of necessity accepted a subordinate status. This subordinatation of the wife satisfied male chauvinism, and several men expressed their dominance by indulging in polygyny and concubinage, though these were more characteristic of the upper classes and less so of the middle classes. In the lower social strata where there were fewer social constraints liaisons of males with a plurality of women were almost as frequent as among the aristocrats.

Having been denied any meaningful role, apart from domestic responsibilities as well as being subjected to the rigours of seclusion and segregation women of all classes in feudal Hyderabad sought compensation at the time of various social and life cycle events. These gave them opportunities to display their ornaments and other fineries. Obviously, then, there was great fondness for ornaments and women were always decked up with an immense amount of jewellery. Several women had as many as seven piercings in each ear, and both sides of the nose had nosepins. In the items of jewellery the things of prime importance were *kali pot ka lachha*—the necklace of black beads put around the women's neck by her mother-in-law at the time of marriage. Bangles too were always worn. Both these were a must for all Muslim women irrespective of their class backgrounds, and parting with either of the two was supposed to bring ill-luck or misfortune.

In matters of dress too, Hyderabadi Muslim women distinguished by their own unique sartorial style. There were neither *ghararas* or *shararra shalwar-kameez* or *chudidar pajamas* as among the North Indian Muslim women. Instead traditional attire consisted of a *pajama* usually of cotton and coloured, a *kurta* always white and of fine *malmal* and *khada-dupatta*, which was as long as a *sari* but was worn in a different style. This style of dressing was undergoing change as we approach the period of Police Action. Thus the *khada-dupatta* was gradually replaced by *saris*. But even along with the *sari*, the same *kurta* was being worn since *blouses* were considered indecent. (Many informants narrated a number of stories about the problems they encountered in changing from *kurta* to blouses.)

Police Action and subsequent events however were to change all this. In fact, fow groups or categories of individuals of the traditional society, were as profoundly affected as women.

Women's Education, and Purdah : The last Nizam Mir Osman Ali Khan took special interest in the popularization of women's education. Along with the Osmania University a Women's College was established. As it was for undergraduates, special arrangements were made at the university for women students who wished to take up postgraduate courses. The informants recalled their university days and narrated some of the interesting details about the segregation of female students in the class-rooms, which were partitioned by a thin wire gauze which neither allowed male students nor teachers to see the girls. Regarding the dress it was to'd that female students wore the typical Hyderabadi dress, and had to keep their heads covered. They did not put on *burqa*.

There were special carriages driven by bullocks called the *shakrams* for female students. These were covered all over and were an important means of transport for school and college going girls. Families affording automobiles sent their daughters to schools and colleges, in them but even these had curtains on the windows. The rich girls never could use the public transport system.

All these examples show that sex segregation was very much present among Hyderabadi Muslims and special arrangements were made to accommodate it. Nonetheless, even respectable families from middle and upper class considered it disgraceful to impose *burqa* or *chadar* on the women (except when they went for *Haj*). It was popular only among the lower classes who could not afford special arrangements for segregation of their women.

Segregation of women was an accepted state policy, therefore in all public places arrangements were available for gender segregation. Details regarding this in the university have been given earlier. In hospitals, shops and even in an annual exhibition which used to be a major event in the civic life of Hyderabad, separate facilities were available for women (Hashmi, 1944).

In hospitals a woman patient could stay in *purdah* and yet get examined by a doctor. Whenever aristocratic women customers were into shops and stores, there were servants along with them to hold white sheets of cloth as they stepped out of the conveyance, whether these were cars, *shakrams* or an *ekka*, and entered the shop in such a way that no males could see them. Once the lady was in the shop curtains were pulled on in such a way that the shopkeeper or the salesman there could not see the woman but she herself could see all that she wanted to purchase.

In the Hyderabad Industrial Exhibition which was organised for a month every year, four or five days were reserved exclusively for women and men were not allowed to enter on those days. This phase of exhibition was known a *zanani numaish.* Once inside, women could move without *Purdah.* After Police Action this facility almost came to an end inasmuch as it got restricted to one day only.

In the above pages on traditional Muslim family and status of women has been dealt with *Purdah,* dress and education of women in the pre-Police Action Hyderabad. This section has not only built up an account of period around Police Action but a little before that, right from the early 20th century to the period around Police Action.

Change in life style and family after Police Action : The economic crisis among Muslims of all classes following the Police Action, brought drastic changes in life style and standard of living. Even elites could not afford their traditional grandeur in their style of life. Renting out their old villas was the only immediate source of income for many middle and upper class families. Some immediate dependents and close relatives were accommodated into small portions which the owners retained for themselves. Many interesting stories about auctions of furniture and decorative items of the nawabs and *Jagirdars* were told during the field work. For several years many ex-aristocrats managed to survive by selling off the family jewellery and utensils. In such circumstances, there was little possibility of hospitality, and guests were not willingly entertained. The feudal tradition of offering hospitality to the guests for days together could not continue any longer. Celebrations like marriages which were occasions for lavish dinners were now over with a simple tea party.

Financial crisis compelled each and every head of the family to earn something in order to support his dependents. This led to the breaking down of the traditional joint families. The decline in affluence discouraged polygamy among the elites. Nor could servants be afforded any more; so servants in elite homes also became a thing of the past. In fact they were even made to vacate the outhouses which once constituted their quarters, so that the ex-masters themselves could live in them. Many examples were narrated where the owners rented out the main building to schools, offices or as halls for the celebrations of marriages and shifted in the outhouses. This became a permanent source for many former aristocrats.

An important point worth mentioning here is that in spite of the economic crisis, Muslims in Hyderabad continued to prefer dependence on jobs (government or private) as was their tradition. However, now as reported by the informants several of the compulsorily retired Muslims or those whose property had been confiscated under the Custodians Property Act, or who had been punished for being found guilty of looting and other corrupt activities, in the pre-Police Action period, and were not left totally helpless, began to turn to petty business. Such individuals started *paan* shops, grocery stores, poultry farms, dairies, and so on. Several individuals also step up some semi-skilled type of services like bicycle repairing, vulcanizing and welding, etc. But such enterprises were often temporary to meet the immediate crisis. Parents saw to it that their children could get higher education, instead of remaining less educated as they had gone. Many children from such families ultimately went abroad for higher education, settled down there and shifted their parents and families.

The institution of family underwent many changes after Police Action, particularly its composition. Joint family was traditionally widespread. Usually the young couple stayed with the husband's parents, though where necessary residence was also taken up with the bride's parents. Nuclear families were rare. This pattern was common in all the three strata. Among the elites the number of dependents was considerably higher than among the other classes as their families included a number of wives, their children, concubines, servants and various other dependents. Details regarding all this have been dealt with in the Chapter on Feudal class structure.

But the post-Police Action financial crisis, informants reported, altered the composition of the Muslim family. Now, polygamy among elites became less frequent and the large families started breaking up. Another reason was that ancestral homes were being disposed of or were being rented for purposes of an income. This factor too began to restrict the size of elite families.

Finding suitable matches from families of similar rank for one's daughters became a problem. In the elite families boys were not well-educated to retain and maintain the social prestige of their forefathers. Therefore they were being considered as unsuitable for the girls of their class. Confronted with this crisis upper class parents started preferring promising and hard working youth from the middle class as husbands for their daughters.

As hypergamous such marriages became widespread, young wives inevitably secured an upper hand over their in-laws and gained a dominant position. This in turn led to a change in the pattern of residence with in-laws, with greater frequency. Thus without any conscious design a change occurred which contributed to the improvement of the position of upper class Muslim women. These are some major changes in family after Police Action.

Another important factor that had a positive effect on women's status was that of dowry. Among the Muslims of Hyderabad dowry demand had always been present and the bride's family was quite proud of the fact that it was in a position to meet the demands of the groom's family. In fact parents wanted to give maximum possible to their daughters even without demanding and marriages became an occasion to flaunt one's wealth. Interestingly, most informants even reported that as Islam denies an equal share to daughters in their father's property, they should be given under the excuse of *Jode-ki-Raqam*. (This was the amount given to the groom by his in-laws for his wedding dress).

But after Police Action when there was an economic crisis, marriages of sons became occasions for acquiring money. Since the girl's family was no longer in a position to offer much voluntarily, the groom's family started demanding it as a matter of right.

Once the migrations began, consequent to the Police Action, there was greater stress on the payment of cash in the name of *Jode-ki-Raqam*. This money was utilized for going abroad. In those cases where one had old family ties or when there was a cousin marriage-dowry or cash could not be easily demanded. In such instances families demanded that the in-laws bear the expenses of sending the groom abroad for higher studies. Such a demand could not be rejected easily, because as has been earlier stated, it was not an easy task to find a match for a daughter, from respectable families with high educational qualifications, after the disintegration of the feudal society. Dowry thus became an instrument to buy the best possible groom for one's daughter. In turn a bride who entered a new family with a lot of dowry in cash and kind, got considerable regard and esteem from her in-laws.

During field work, researcher learnt of many instances where marriages were settled on the condition that after the engagements the girl's parents would bear the expenses of the groom's foreign study trip marriage took place after the boy completed the education and settled down with a job. A few exceptional cases were also reported in which the boys did not prove worthy of the trust placed in them, and they married and settled down abroad.

Women employment : One important impact of Police Action was that women became earning memberes specially as teachers. Due to the losr of traditional incomes, many families, who had huge houses, established private schools on their premises, and thus provided job opportunities to famale graduates, particular to those belonging to middle and lower classes. Thus a process of pulling women out of traditional domestic roles was initiated by the sheer compulsion of the socio-economic circumstances following Police Action.

A few lower middle class Muslim women also entered poultry farming and the like, to meet the economic crisis. Their ultimate objective in this was to help their children acquire higher education, and attain respectable jobs. Many examples were quoted to illustrate how parents worked hard to send their children to USA for higher education.

The important point worth noting here is that the economic crisis following Police Action necessitated an important change in the feudal value system. Women's employment which traditionally was a taboo, got acceptance, thus necessitating women's education. In spite of the fact that the *purdah* arrangements could not continue in schools, colleges, university and offices, yet Muslims responded to the situation by educating their daughters. Educated daughters meant increased family income, easy marriageability but over and above an enlightened younger generation as well.

Change in Life Style and Retraditionalization due to Overseas Employment

The most favourite use of petrodollars has been purchase of real estate and thereafter the repairs and reconditioning of the old houses. However, the neorich lacking the sophistication of the feudal elites and aristocrats are unable to decorate their houses tastefully. During field work it was observed that while externally the houses were very well repaired and painted, internally they were not. The furniture and the decorations were loud, garish and ostentatious, revealing the lack of refinement and good taste. In fact, from the internal decorations and furniture, the researcher could reasonably guess for how many generations a particular family had a tradition of maintaining a drawing room.

Besides drawing rooms, kitchens too indicate affluence with many of them being full of modern gadgets. But questioning revealed that few of these are actually used, since the technical aspects of electric gadgets are neither understood nor fully mastered by those who have only recently acquired the means to own gadgets. Thus, these are more status symbols than objects of utility and conveniences.

Owning a vehicle for personal use has always been a matter of great prestige. Prior to the inflow of patrodollars, for many middle class individuals ownership of even a mere motor cycle was a matter of pride; while owning a car was a symbol of great prosperity and prestige among Hyderabadi Muslims. Interestingly, a similar situation still prevails. Though many can now afford cars, yet, two wheelers are very popular—scooters and motor cycles among the youth and and moped among the elderly.

Irrespective of class, most Hyderabadi Muslims today own television sets. But since the local transmission is in Telugu, they mostly watch the national programmes relayed from Delhi. The "video culture" has become very popular, and families enjoy watching movies for hours together. Video-watching has also become an occasion for social gatherings.

Such gatherings have become a matter of prestige for the person who arranges these shows at his residence. Video recordings of marriage celebrations is also very common. These video cassettes are eventually sent to the family members who are abroad. Recorded messages on audio cassettes are also sent to relatives living in foreign countries. A large number of Muslims have also established video parlours in the city; these are doing brisk business.

One of the leading reasons for extravagance is that the Muslims had never been in business or commerce and as such, had never realized the virtue of thrift. Being a part of feudal society for ages, Muslims had a nostalgic longing for those days, after they had lost their elitist position in 1948. Thus it was very easy for them to succumb to conspicuous consumption and consumerism, when the rotating wheel of fortune gave them an opportunity. The researcher found this to be generally true of all the Muslims irrespective of their class—lower, middle or upper.

Consistent with feudal values, to be considered as "well off" has always been a strong desire among Hyderabadi Muslims. Field work revealed that to achieve this objective, individuals spend a lot of money on lavish celebration of occasions of minor importance. Inviting people at home for dinners has become a common practice now. The number of invitees and the quality of food is something to boast about. Events like *Daswan* (the tenth day) or *Chehlum* (the fortieth day) of death have become occasions for inviting as many relatives and friends as possible, alongwith the poor and needy, and serving sumptuous dinners. Two examples from the researcher's family are worth illuminating. The first of these was where one of her distant relatives spent some nineteen thousand rupees in 1986 to organise the most lavish *Chehlum* dinner to feed a virtual army of friends, relatives others. The other example is that of the *Chehlum* dinner of the researcher's own grand mother, for which some five hundred people were invited for the occasion, in spite of the fact that none of her relatives is in the Gulf, remitting petrodollars. But since such observances have become the norm it is socially improper not to observe such occasions on a lavish scale.

Such examples indicate that several values and practices that were a part of the feudal culture and which had disappeared after Police Action, have now resurfaced. Extravagant spending on joyous occasions like *Aqiqa*, *Bismillah* and birthdays etc. have become so essential that people do not hesitate to sell off their gold ornaments, television sets or transistors for meeting the expenses. An example to which the researcher has been an eye witness is that in Hyderabad, a Muslim organisation called "Toor Bait-ul-Mal", which offers loans without interest on the basis of some tangible security. On her visits to the office of this organisation, the researcher observed many *burqa* clad ladies with gold ornaments, big transistors and even television sets mortaging these items in order to berrow money for meeting the expenses of such events as *Aqiqa*, birthdays, engagements and even *Chehlum*. Presumably these people had for long been deprived of their needs and their enjoyment since Police Action. Now that they have some money at their disposal the temptation to spend and enjoy seems to be irresistible. Indeed, so strongly have they succumbed to the temptation of enjoying life that they have rendered themselves incapable of saving out of their income so as to be able to afford some luxuries at a future date, or to provide for security in old age.

Eating outside of homes is fast becomiug a widespread habit. Thanks to their Muslim customers, both men and women, restaurants are doing roaring business. Prior to the inflow of petrodollars, restaurants were the monopoly of Iranians, but now local Muslims have also entered into this line. There are certain establishments which are famous for special preparations. One has to wait for quite some time before being served. One such example is a *chakna* shop at Gunfoundry.

Changing Position of Women due to Overseas Employment

At least one sociological study (Saiyed, 1976) has shown that the position of Muslim women is very high, when the menfolk are earning abroad, leaving the responsibility of managing the household and the remittances to women. In Hyderabad too, overseas employment has had a profound impact on the position especially of middle class Hyderabadi Muslim women since the earning male members in several families are away, giving women an opportunity to independently manage family responsibilities and household affairs. During her field work the researcher observed that as a consequence of this absence of male heads women had come to enjoy substantial power in the household and there is reason to believe that in many clases young wives are now in a position to dominate their mothers-in-law. Field work revealed that while the husbands were away women preferred staying with their own parents rather than their in-laws. Because of this the remittance drafts from abroad were being received by wives in their parental homes while this is, for obvious reasons, causing tension between wives and their in-laws, living with parents rather than parents-in-law has given women, apart from personal freedom, abundant spending power. Both these have led to a change in women's life-style. It is now easier for them to move out of home with their friends, without having to encounter objections or criticisms of the in-laws. Besides, when children have gone to school and the domestic servants are there to look after domestic chores, women are free to visit shopping centres, go for picnics and movies, etc. This freedom, middle class Muslim women are enjoying for the first time.

A large number of beauty parlours have sprung up in the city; visiting these has become a regular feature of women's lives as they have ecough time and resources to spend on themselves. Beauticians have become a must for bridal make-up irrespective of class. The girls working in these parlours have a lot of clients with whom they also deal privately at home. A number of elegant hair styles are in fashion; however there is an aversion for having hair cuts in western style, particularly among the lower classes and middle classes. Patronage of beauty parlours represents a radical change from the traditions of pre-petrodollar Hyderabad in which women of middle class had never dreamt of going out of their homes for purpose of personal beautification.

Similarly, among women of lower middle class families also there is now greater personal freedom and less constraints on their enjoyment of life. In families of this strata, women have virtually become movie crazy, since movie going is the cheapest pastime. This is the class which cannot afford video cassette recorders at home. In almost every movie theatre in Hyderabad, a large number of *burqa* clad women are seen; *burqa* incidentally is a symbol of these classes, and has been affected by modernization. Passing time has become a real problem for these women. In the course of interview with the researcher these women expressed how proud they were about having seen all the movies running in a city at a particular time.

The oil boom has introduced a peculiar pattern of emigration among the women of lower classes, who have been the worst victims of *jagirdari* abolition after Police Action. Oil buyouncy however came to their rescue in a strange way. The Arabs who had settled down in Hyderabad started renewing their old home ties and migrating back to their homeland to take advantage of new opportunities there. But, due to their age long contacts with Hyderabadi society, they still continued the practice of marrying Hyderabadi wives.

Among Arabs it is customary for a man to pay a handsome amount of dower to marry a girl. This custom has made marriages of males difficult in Arab societies. The dower however is not so high among Indian Muslims. Now when the Arabs residing in Arab countries saw Arabs of Hyderabad returning and bringing along with them Hyderabadi Muslim wives, for whom they did not pay much dower, they also thought of marrying girls from Hyderabad. Initially, the lower class Arabs, who were totally strangers to Hyderabad but could afford little dower, got their marriages fixed through the ex-Hyderabad based migrating Arab families. The possibility of such alliance encouraged the poorer families in Hyderabad to give their daughters in marriage to such Arabs. But in a short while this phenomenon, which originally started due to the genuine needs of both parties, became a situation of exploitation. As already stated, such Indo-Arab marriages, in the first instance, began with the migrating families serving as middlemen. But realizine the money making potential of the situation, exploitative brokers came into existence in the city and transformed marriage into a business. Attractive sums of money were offered to lower class parents in exchange for their daughters. Succumbing to the temptations, poor parents started getting rid of their daughters without considering the age, health and economic position of the bridegroom. Indeed, they were not even careful to see if these were genuine marriages. Their only concern was the money they got. Many rickshaw pullers, domestic servants began to make hay while the sun shone and brought scandal and notoriety to the entire community.

The research made a special probe into this situation by investigating 30 lower class families of whom at present: 10 were beggars, 10 were rickshaw pullers and 10 were domestic servants. The monthly income of family averaged from Rs. 150 to 500, and the average size of the honsehold was 8. Investigation into family histories revealed that 12 out of these 30 families had been originally dependent on *jagirdars*, dut were now rickshaw pullers or beggars. 7 of these 30 ramilies were themselves members of *jagirdar* families and had once supported many poor dependents but were now reduced to utter poverty. Today, 5 heads of families out of these 7 were unemployed and were without any source of income; they could not even manage two square meals a day for the family. The remaining 4 families were direct victims of Police Action in the rural areas of Bidar and Osmanabad and settled down in Hyderabad as domestic servants. All these 30 families had married of atleast one of their daughters to Arabs, who incidentally are referred to as "Sheikhs" by the poor Muslims, even though the concerned Arab may himself be a poor man in his own country. Such has been the opiating effect of these marriages.

A further probe revealed that out of the 30 girls given away in marriage to Arabs 8 had been victims of desertion by their Indian husbands and 4 were widows.

This investigation was further supplemented by collecting information from the Passport Office, where such marriages have to be registered for the purpose of obtaining a passport to emigrate from India. The information of the Passport Office, and interviews with the Passport Officer, revealed that on an average 20 to 25 marriages were registered every month in 1985. This office further revealed that the age difference between the husband and wife was 20 to 45 years.

Usually these girls were taken as second and third wives. Out of the 30 cases discussed above, 10 girls were married to handicapped men (4 blind, 2 deaf and dumb, 3 lame and 1 with an amputated arm). This investigative probe established the fact that these marriages took place due to the poverty of the girls' parents.

Brokers play an important role in these marriages. Indeed, in some cases the parents even had no direct contact with the so-called bridgegroom; the brokers finalized the deal and collected the commission from both aides. The parents got an amount ranging between 10 to 15 thousand rupees depending on the age and health of the groom.

The researcher further found that such marriages occurred without any consent of the concerned girls, which really makes such alliances un-Islamic. But since they provide financial support to the poor families no attention is paid to the religious injunctions. The parents openly admitted that from the money they so obtained, they got their other daughters married off, and/or started a small *paan*-shop, or bought a cycle rickshaw for their sons which guaranteed two square meals a day for the whole of the family. In some cases, the girls who were married off to Arabs were able to secure jobs for their brothers in West Asia, which, in turn, positively influenced the entire family's economic condition. Incidentally, the securing of a job for a male relative, specially brother, means an additional security for the girls in the foreign land.

Cases were reported where girls, ostensibly taken abroad as wives, were sold after being divorced. In some cases, when these girls became widows, their relations did not treat them well and deprived them of their share in the property, once again this was done in violation of the Islamic laws of inheritance. The researcher came across some cases where one Arab man married three to four girls one after another and left all of them behind promising to send their visa after reaching his country. But the visas never turned up. And neither were these "wives" getting any maintenance from their husband, nor were they free to remarry. When the parents were interviewed they expressed regret and sorrow over such injustices but also expressed their helplessness and stated that they were forced to more or less "sell" away their daughters under the compulsion of circumstances.

Marriage and dowry: Marriage ceremonies of Hyderabad had always been memorable; thanks to petrodollars they now rival, if not exceed, the scale of feudal times. The extravagance begins with the invitation cards on which a considerable expenditure is incurred. They are printed in beautifully decorated patterns, and are distributed in large numbers. Marriage halls are booked well in advance and illuminated with coloured lights even before the actual marriage day. Lavish dinners are served to guests. Indeed, the number of dishes have become a symbol of prestige. Alongwith innumerable dishes of both Hyderabadi and Western style, at least three to four types of sweet dishes are also served. Bridegrooms are taken to the place of marriage in imported cars even if they have to be hired at a cost Rs. 500 to 1000. This amount is spent for a short trip not lasting for more than half an hour. The cars are decorated with flowers which cost around one thousand rupees. All this is in addition to the heavy expenditure on the purchase of cloth, gold and jewellery.

As mentioned elsewhere in this book, there had been a traditional practice of paying a large amount of money to the groom by the parents of the girl called "*Jode-ki-Raqam*". This payment still continues but now consists of exhorbitive amount which vary according to the academic qualifications and the job of the groom. Those who are western qualified, or are employed in UK, USA or in any of the western Asian countries have a much higher rate. The family background of the grooms is no barrier for obtaining large payments as "*Jode-ki-Raqam*". Informants/respondents revealed that it was not unusual for those members of their families who were abroad to get as much as 25 to 40 thousand rupees under this arrangement.

The occasion of *Nikah* (marriage contract) is preceded and followed by a number of traditional ceremonies like the *manja, sanckak, mehndi*, before marriage; all these had almost lost their significance since the disintegration of the feudal order, but are again being celebrated with traditional enthusiasm and extravagance. The only change which the researcher now observed is in *chauthi* and *walima*, the two dinners given by the bride's family and the groom's family respectively; these have now been merged into one and the expenditure is jointly shared by the two parties, also now, in most cases, the traditional *jumaqi* dinners are omitted, not for reasons of economy but because marriages are hurriedly settled and the grooms with or without the brides leave for their overseas jobs within a week or ten days after the marriage.

Thus marriages have become occasions of hectic activity, great expenditure and also a lot of enjoyment and celebration like feudal marriages were.

Beside the ceremony of marriage there are numerous other marriage linked functions which are also extravagantly celebrated. These average at least twice a week. One either is attending some of the other function at some relative's house or is himself arranging a get together at his own home. Thus as in feudal times, present day marriages for many Hyderabadi Muslims have become a merrry-go-round of ceremonies and functions.

To conclude an enquiry into the details of match making among Hyderabadi Muslims it can be said that marriage is not simply the forging of a bond between two individuals. Rather it is more a channel of upward mobility from one's present social position. In this respect both the younger generation and the older generation have the same views and attitude with some possible exceptions among youngmen holding overseas jobs for whom money is no problem. Their interest is in a lavish and ostentatious marriage solemnized in the best and costliest marriage hall, like for example, the exhibition club or Eden Garden (Palace of the Queen of the last Nizam), Lady Hyderi Club and other similar prestigious locations.

As has been repeatedly pointed out, dowry has been a very important feature of Muslim marriages in Hyderabad, being equally prevalent in all classes. Exceptions however were found among a microscopic minority which had come under the influence of the Jamat-e-Islami. But the Jamat's resistance to dowry has not inspired Hyderabadi Muslims because there is a widespread belief that the followers of the Jamat do not care for the sanctity of marriage and may divorce their wives or indulge in a multiple marriage, since polygamy commonly considered improper is an acceptable concept among these people. Therefore, the researcher found that only poor people gave their daughters in marriage to the followers of the Jamat, and these people are in no position to give dowry. On the other hand, it was found that, by and large, the informants and respondents interviewed were in favour of dowry, as discussed in detail earlier.

In present times with the Gulf money pouring in, dowry is considered as the best "investment" for the better future of the girls by their parents. An attractive dowry means a good son-in-law, and a good son-in-law means a stable married life for the daughter. Dowry varied according to the education and the job of the groom. Technically qualified boys command much more than others. At the time of data collection (1983-85) it ranged from ten thousand rupees to one lakh rupees according to the socio-economic standing of the families involved. Apart from the payment of cash, dowry includes immobile property, car, scooter, and other durable assets. Immobile property is generally passed on in the name of the bride. This brings her a lot of status and respect in the groom's family. Remarkably enough. many respondents of the study defended the giving of dowry to daughters by saying that since Islam did not provide equal share in inheritance to the sons and daughters, the latter must be compensated through payment of dowry. The point however was overlooked that dowry really went to the son-in-law and not the daughter.

In the middle class families, today, technical professional qualifications have become desirable in the daughter-in-law. Should a doctor or an engineer daughter-in-law become available, several other considerations including dowry are overlooked. One interesting observation that needs to be noted concerning negotiations on dowry is that the parents of eligible bachelors, employed abroad, were more interested in this matter than their sons. The parents feel that since their sons were earning handsomely abroad, they deserved to get a substantial dowry. Consequently, they do a great deal of "shopping around" for satisfactory dowry, and try to squeeze out as much as they can from the girls' parents in the form of cash, furniture, jewellery, clothes, utensils, immobile property like plots of land and houses and mobile property like scooter, motor cycle and bicycle. All these are left behind with the groom's parents when he returns overseas.

But, interviews with several grooms revealed that their main concern was the girl's appearance and in many cases even her education and employment or family background were ignored if she was extraordinarily beautiful. Obviously, where youngmen are willing to forego dowry for the sake of other considerations there is friction between them and their parents.

The case of bachelors employed in Hyderabad or elsewhere in India is different. While they too wish to obtain dowry, they simultaneously give consideration to her education and employment potential as well—factors which are absent in case of men employed abroad. Unlike the latter, youngmen employed in India itself have a limited source of income hence they want wives who can supplement their income. Wherever possible they try to enter alliance into influential families so that the contacts of their in-law can prove helpful in seeking jobs or promotion.

Role of Women in Rise of Consumerism : It would be evident to any field workers in the Muslim *mohallas* that from morn to dusk there is brisk business being transacted in clothing, jewellery and bangle stores; these stores are overflowing with Muslim women. Thus in the increasing consumerism that now characterizes the Muslims' changing life style it is women who are playing an important role. Remittances have whetted the appetite for ornaments and jewellery among Muslim women in the lower and middle classes. (The substantial profits from this brisk business however are being reaped by Marwadis).

There is considerable competitiveness among women in the exhibition of their ornaments. But apart from gold ornaments there is a craze for latest fashions in dress and bangles, especially for traditional Hyderabadi stone bangles known as *Nagon Ke Jode*. Each set costs upto one thousand rupees or even more. These are usually worn on occasions like marriages, and ceremonies that precede and follow marriages. It is not unusual for a woman to possess four to five such sets so that she may wear different sets during the week long celebrations. These bangles are also very much in demand among Hyderabadis who are in the Gulf, or those settled in UK, USA, Canada, etc.

Many new stores have come up to cater to the needs of women, and the size of exclusive ladies corners in the existing shops have been enlarged and decorated. Shopkeepers and merchants show polite hospitality and offer tea or cold drinks to the customers. Though the centre for all purchases is the Old City around Charminar and Gulzar house but it is a symbol of prestige to buy jewellery from expensive jewellers like Musaddi Lal or Chhagan Lal in the new city commercial complexes of Bashir Bagh and Abids.

8

Conclusion

Introduction

Although the partition of the country was in many respects a disaster for the Muslims of divided India, the tragedy of Hyderabadi Muslims in serveral respects has been more serious one. Unlike the North Indian Muslims who had lost power to the British more than a century ago, Hyderabadi Muslims continued to be the ruling elite even after India was partitioned in 1947. But following the dissolution of Asaf Jahi dynasty in 1948, they overnight suffered a role reversal and lost their pre-eminent position in the state, power and dominance, and alongwith these, the society and culture that had been built over a period of six centuries rapidly distintegrated. For Hyderabadi Muslims, whether they belonged to the elite class or the masses, glory evaporated into nothingness in the course of just one fateful week in September 1948 when India initiated Police Action for the integration of the state into Indian Union. The state of Hyderabad which remained under Muslim supremacy for about five centuries i.e. 1518—1948 became a part of Indian Republic with a Hindu based polity, though of course, within the secular framework of its Constitution.

Inevitably, on account of their elitist position, the Hyderabadi Muslims developed a distinct ethos was very different from the Indo-Muslim culture that had developed in North India as a result of more than six centuries of Mughal rule. The Deccani or Hyderabadi Muslim culture was a synthesis of the royal cultures of Iran, which the Qutub Shahis had brought with them, the Mughal culture brought by the Mughal subedar and the Hindu culture of Dravadian origin. Synthetic culture was a notable feature of social life of Hyderabad prevailing over generations of Muslim rule. Here an example from the period of Mir Mahboob Ali Khan Asaf Jah VI is worth mentioning.

At the time of disastrous floods in 1908 when a number of people lost not only their lives but their homes belongings even Muslims did not hesitate to perform *puja* to the river and propitiate the angry Goddess, on the advice of the Brahmin pandits. A golden tray containing *sari*, pearls, yellow rice, red *kumkum* coconuts encased in gold and silver and a lamp were arranged for *puja*. Mir Mahboob Ali Khan Asaf Jah VI is reported to have gone on horse back in the pouring rain into the swirling waters and performed *puja* and *arti* (Lynton and Rajan, 1974 : 16).

Apart from the cultural synthesis another important thing was the importance of the king and his patronage in the social life. Even in the late forties when the whole subcontinent was nearing independence, the people of Hyderabad could not imagine their existence without the Nizam who was a legendary figure for them. Every week in the *kutba* of Friday prayers he was called "Khaladallhul-Mulk-O-Saltanat" (the unchallenged owner of the state) and "Zil-ullah" (the shadow of God). The Nizam was considered something super human.

Even the opposition parties which were totally against the Nizam's government, in their memorandum of demands began with an expression of loyalty and prayers for the long life of the Nizam. All this very obviously shows that the people of Hyderabad could not imagine their existence without the Nizam, and his patronage in spite of all his shortcomings.

After 1947 the relations between the Hindu and Muslims became so bitter that all these examples became unbelievable. The *Majlis* continued its unequivocal support to the continuation of Muslim rule in Hyderabad. Congress and other Hindu parties were opposing Muslim supremacy. This clash of interests reached to such a climax that a Hindu fanatic attempted on Nizam's life and threw a bomb on his car on December 4, 1947 when he was coming out of King Kothi in his daily visit to *Kilwat* (Rehber-e-Deccan 5th December, 1947).

With all his benevolence, and repeated proclamations that Hindus and Muslims were like his two eyes the Nizam could not enjoy the support of Hindu subjects as a monarch. The Hindu felt that they could no more continue with the traditional values of surrendering their rights to a benevolent monarch. All this shows that the clash of interest could in no time polarise the Hindus and Muslims in spite of all the communal harmony that existed over generations.

The inevitable occurred and the government of India had no other alternative and was compelled for a Police Action which started on 13th September and completed on 17th September 1948. A Muslim stata which was eventually carved in the South by the different dynasties of Bahminis, Qutub Shahis and Asaf Jahi was brought in the mainstream of united India. A distinct culture of the area was taken away its boundaries. A peculiar social order which was nurtured under of benevolent kings of three different dynasties lost its peculiarities under the new changes. A state which proved to be an island of peace and security during the freedom struggle of 1857 for all the Indians was now at the mercy of decision at Delhi.

The Police Action was a dividing landmark for the age long memorable cultural integrity and communal harmony. Hindu community suffered for a few months before Police Action by the repression of the *Razakars* which the Nizam failed to control, partly in his own interest and party the situation went out of his control. But after Police Action the whole Muslim community had to reap the results for the decades, of those few fanatics who could not foresee the repercussions. It was revenged within a fortnight for what the *Razakars* had done in years. Muslim masses became the victims of brutality and humiliation and were thrown on the streets homeless. *Purdash* observing females were humiliated, raped and killed.

Immediately afterwards there was a challenge of survival for the Muslims due to the disintegration of the feudal order.

Abolition of the *jagirs* and retrenchment of Muslims from services turned them into paupers. A few migrated to Pakistan but it did not solve the problem of the majority of Muslims' They stayed back in Hyderabad alongwith the Nizam who decided to stay back in the land of his forefathers, even after the loss of power.

The period following Police Action is marked by a vacuum of any historical or sociological work bringing out the disintergation and plight of Police Action, except a few academic and non-academic works mentioned in the survey of literature. Therefore the present study has tried to fulfil this gap. It is perhaps one of the first studies with two important features. Firstly, it takes into account the differential impact of change on all the three different strata of the society i.e. upper, middle and lower. Another important feature of this study is that it covers a very vast canvas beginning with the pre-Police Action grandeur, the plight of Police Action, the gloom and disintegration that followed Police Action, and finally the changes in contemporary Muslim society due to oil boom of the Gulf and the remittances pouring into Hyderabad city.

As any study of social change requires a two time dimensional picture in order to have a clear understanding of the state in which a particular society, community or group existed at the time of initiation of change and where it has landed after that change, and as social change is a continuous phenomenon involving number of political and economic aspects of a society alongwith that of social aspects. Therefore, a research in social change covers a vast canvas taking into consideration various social, political and economic factors responsible for a particular type of social change in a particular society, community or a group. So has been the case with present research. It is a study dealing with Hyderabadi Muslims, a once dominant, ethnic grouping which continued its supremacy till a very recent past i.e. 1948.

The specific objectives of the study (as specified in the introduction earlier) were to build an account of traditional culture and society of Hyderabadi Muslims, so that a clear picture of socio-economic and socio-political impact of partition and Police Action upon Hyderabadi Muslims could emerge.

The next important aspect of the present study was to analyse the kind and extent of change and modernization that is being reflected in social life and to evaluate the role of remittance economy in this change.

Another important feature of the present study has been to examine these impacts and response as they have affected the various social strata of the Muslim community rather than giving a generalized one because of the now well known theoretical position that change and modernization impinge differentially upon different social groups and classes.

In dealing with such a vast panorama of change, which of necessity had to be of a macro character, the study was faced with a methodological challenge, which was all the more acute because of an almost total dearth of secondary sources and any other literature on the subject.

To meet this situation, certain unusual steps were taken. First, field work consisted of intensive interviews with about 125 informants with whose assistance an "oral historical account" was constructed. Due to the unusually large number of informants who were interviewed, the problem of reliability of data was overcome since checking and cross-checking could be done. Second, to further enhance confidence in the data a micro survey of 160 families was undertaken. Thus the "oral histories" of the informants, the life histories of the respondents and the participant observations of the respondents and the participant observations of the researcher herself constituted the three legged stool on which the data of present study rests.

In this survey data was collected on three different time dimensions which the study has spanned. Information regarding three successive generations in each family was obtained so that a clear picture of social change concerning various aspects of change i.e. intergenerational mobility due to professional education and change in occupational structure, migration to west and then finally due to overseas employment could emerge. The findings of this micro analysis supported the macro-level observation to a substantial extent.

As stated earlier an important precondition of the study of change is an indepth understanding of life and socio-economic and socio-cultural conditions at the time of initiation of change. So it was very important to build up a detailed account of the traditional feudal social order and Muslim culture at the time of Police Action, from where onwards new trends of change evolved including the challenge of adjustment of new socio-political conditions.

Accordingly the various phases of the present research were :

(a) Historical account of Muslim ascendancy in Hyderabad.
(b) Socio-political account and a profile of traditional feudal system.
(c) Police Action and aftermath—The challenge of adjustment in the new political set-up—migrations to the western countries.
(d) The Gulf boom—Overseas Employment and its Impact.
(e) A survey of 3 generations in 160 purposively sampled families on such dimensions.

Findings : The main findings of the study are related to the examination of the aftermath of the Police Action, employment opportunities in the Gulf and the survey of three generations in 160 families. In each of these themes we have seen the impact of the two exogenous factors, namely, Police Action and the Gulf boom, and the response that the Hyderabadi Muslims have shown to these factors of change.

One special contribution of the present study has been to examine these impacts and responses as they have affected the various social strata of the Muslim community rather than in terms of generalization for the entire community. This has been done because of the now well known theoretical position that change and modernization impinge differentially upon different social groups and classes.

With the above clarification, we first discuss our findings pertaining to the aftermath of Police Action.

Police Action brought about a total upheaval in the Muslim feudal society for Hyderabad. In terms of class its deepest impact was felt by the feudal aristocracy and the lower classes, especially the unskilled among them.

Impact on feudals : For the upper class aristocracy the political turn of events was an extremely shocking experience. By and large, it had failed to read the writing on the wall and was therefore psychologically unprepared for a situation in which it stood deprived completely of its elitist status and power. To aggravate matters, the aristocracy had never given importance to education and professional careers therefore it was academically ill-equipped to adjust to the new order and to the new scheme of things. In such cataclasmic change, the only option this class had was withdrawal and following withdrawal it sunk into stagnation.

Impact on middle class : Initially middle class Muslims also found the changes ushered in by Police Action to be overwhelming. Individuals and families belonging to this section of society were also gripped with fear and insecurity. However, eventual adjustment and response was more positive in this case because the middle class Muslims in Hyderabad placed strong value on education. Traditionally what little mobility could be achieved in the ascription dominated feudal society was only on the basis of education. This tradition of education was now to serve individuals in this strata well. In fact many in such families were now able to perceive greater opportunities for mobility through education. In course of time therefore the response to change in this class turned out to be, as has been said earlier, positive. In fact, the period following Police Action turned out to be a period of awakening insofar as new opportunities were concerned.

Impact on the lower class : Like the upper class, Police Action also had a negative impact on the lower classes. The Muslim lower classes who had always been social parasites and dependents on the feudal families were also adversely affected. They had no skill and were totally dependent on support of the feudal class in the form of domestic service or being attached to them. Hence they were forced into begging and became the victims of many social evils.

As is evident from the data of the microview, of the three strata the middle class Muslims either retained their social status or even managed to climb up on the social ladder.

The next important finding was that Police Action led to several migrations. The economic and political role reversal following the post-Police Action plight led to migrations of Muslims from Hyderabad. The lead in this matter was provided by the prominent *Razakar* leaders and others who were in responsible positions in the Nizam's government at the time of Police Action. This migration was of a permanent nature. However, the fact that the Nizam unlike the Nawab of Junagarh did not run away from the state, stabilized the Muslim community and the early fears of large scale migration did not materialize. This was an important development inasmuch as the vast majority of Hyderabadi Muslims decided to stay back. This decision was eventually to influence the pattern of their subsequent adjustment.

There then began another wave of migrations, which was not for political reasons. These migrations were to the west, rather than to Pakistan. The qualitative difference between the two was that those who went to the west could maintain their links with the native soil, and return home whenever they wanted. Also, a part of their affluence came back to Hyderabad and altered the perspectives and outlooks of those who had stayed behind this wave of migration that started in the decade of mid-fifties and was much more influential in bringing about certain permanent changes in family, education, profession, status of women, life-style and religiosity. All this has been dealt with in detail in the study. What may however be mentioned here is that the possibility of migration to western countries served as a great incentive for acquiring education. Prior to Police Action a profession was not of a value for the aristocratic families as it meant an instrumental utilization of one's acquired knowledge. But this resistance was to change. In the middle class too, the urge for professional education received a big boast since it opened up the doors of migration.

The last Nizam had done a great deal to popularize female education. The financial crisis that followed Police Action, gave a further impetus to women's education. Muslim women particularly in the middle class were compelled to come out of *purdah* and take up suitable jobs to supplement family income. This subsequently was to prove beneficial for the modernization of the Hyderabadi Muslim family.

However, on the whole the Police Action had given a great setback to the Muslim community. In about no time the Muslims lost all their glory, power and affluence which had been built over a period of almost five centuries. Undoubtedly, efforts to adjust continued but partly because of the relative absence of opportunities and partly due to the presence of prejudice and discrimination, it was not easy to come to terms with the new situation. The study has touched upon the deterioration in the quality of life as an aftermath of Police Action; this deterioration was particularly marked in the case of the aristocrats and the elites. But apart from this, the traditional ways of life, the exuberant celebrations of festivals, the long and extravagant modes of marriage ceremonies and rituals, the spacious housing all gradually vanished for most sections of Hyderabadi Muslims.

This part of our analysis ends by observing that the Hyderabadi Muslims, in general, had been overcome by a sense of deep frustration, even though at the individual level some persons did struggle to overcome the crisis in which the community had been enveloped.

After this, the study moved on to the next important development which affected the subjects under study, namely, oil boom which began in 1970s. This development brought much needed relief to Hyderabadi Muslims; it opened up opportunities of employment and made possible for large numbers the remittance of petrodollars. The Muslims of Hyderabad now entered a new phase of social change.

Accordingly, the third part of the study has documented in detail the impact of petrodollars, particularly upon women and family. The main findings of this unforeseen prosperity have been (1) Improvement in Standard of Life and Consumerism, (2) Retraditionalization (3) Improvement in the status of women in upper class and middle class families, but a decline in status of women in the lower classes, (4) Communal friction, and rise of fundamentalism, (5) Preference for technical and professional education and loss of interest in higher education among the middle class. These findings are briefly recapitulated blow.

(1) *Improvement in Standard of Life, Rise of Consumerism and Retraditionalization*: It has been pointed out in the concerned chapter that thanks to the almost unlimited employment opportunities enjoyed by Hyderabadi Muslims in the Gulf countries, a sea change has occurred in their standard of life. Alongwith this has come an almost unbridled consumerism.

While the above mentioned developments have been along expected lines, a somewhat unusual finding has been the emergence of retraditionalization of Hyderabadi culture, as well.

In retrospect, it now appears that it was perhaps only natural for an ex-feudal society, with its memories of past glory still alive to go back to its old traditions, which it had cherished with nostalgic longings, as soon as it regained economic security. Thus, today, not only the ex-feudal elites but all sections of Hyderabadi Muslim society are retreating into the "good old days". This is particularly to be seen in the display of a lavish life-style and the extravagant celebration of festivals, marriages, and so on. Given money and affluence, Hyderabadis are indulging in luxuries they had once known. Even those who were never a part of the feudal aristocracy are today vicariously enjoying the psychological pleasure of feudal elitism. Modern consumerism, our observations have led us to conclude, are the observe side of feudal extravagance, and a mechanism that facilitates retraditionalization.

However, in case of the lower class Muslims, our data has shown that the improvement in their condition has not been all that remarkable.

Status of women: On this dimension the findings have been mixed, with socio-economic class again providing the differential. For the upper and the middle class women, handsome earnings of their husbands overseas have been a boon and has affected their status. In the absence of their husbands, (who are serving abroad) it was women who were found to plan their family expenditures, savings, children's education, etc. These new responsibilities have given a self-confidence to Muslim women which they have traditionally not known. However, attention has also been drawn in these towards various family frictions that are arising due to affluence.

But regarding women of lower class, present finding is that the oil boom has been quits a curse. It is they who are taken to Gulf countries as wives and subjected to all sorts of tortures. A number of them have been married to aged, handicapped men who already have wives and a large number of children. These poor girls are just married in order to serve them and their other wives in old age. At times they just divorce them or sell them off or when the husband dies these ill-fated girls are not treated well by his grown-up sons and wives.

Rise of fundamentalism and communal friction: Another finding (though detailed attention has not given to this) was that the new prosperity of Muslims has been viewed by the Hindu majority to be threatening. This insecurity has been aggravated by the rise of fundamentalism and political manouvrings. So one negative impact of prosperity has been the aggravation of communal friction, in a society which had historically been characterised by relative inter-communal understanding and co-existence.

Change in educational attainments: Since the opening up of job opportunities in the Gulf, Muslims in Hyderabad have been interested in those courses that would fetch them handsome salaries in the Gulf. As the professional courses assure independent means of earning a livelihood here in India and better salaries in the Gulf they are the first preferênce. Courses like M.B. B.S., B.E., diploma in engineering or post-graduate in agriculture, pharmacy, genetics, microbiology, biochemistry or computer courses are very popular among Muslim youth these days. Those coming from the middle class also aspire such courses but on failing to get admission there they prefer, like many students from lower classes to turn to vocational courses like typing and shorthand, draughtsman, cooling and refrigeration, etc. rather than opting for a liberal arts college education which their parents had done in search of government job. Informants in the Osmania University have pointed out that this attitude has affected Muslim enrolment in social sciences, humanities, languages and commerce. In the lower class families too, youth who have never had any occupational skills are now interested in learning trades like welding, tailoring, driving rather than seeking unskilled government jobs as peons, postmen, watchmen and police constables, etc. which their fathers had done.

Field work also revealed that there now exists even among the Muslims of lower class background a craze for English medium schools. But due to thelack of compatibility between the environment at home and at school, there is a high rate of school dropouts. This is indicative of the fact that English education cannot be relied upon as a channel of mobility for lower class Muslims.

To summarize, then, our findings clearly show that in their adjustment and response to change, Hyderabadi Muslims have not shown one uniform pattern; rather their reactions have been in terms of the socio-economic strata to which they have belonged. This observation has two important theoretical implications. First, it confirms that the response to change by any group or community is not uniform. Second, it also confirms that even a community like the Muslims, which in the perspective of majority-minority relations, is often perceived as a monolith, has deep inter-community variations that are influenced by the existential conditions of the various sections of the community.

Limitations: As has been pointed out in more than one place in this book, there exists a virtual vacuum of empirical studies in the period following Independence. This paucity of studies served for obvious reasons and in obvious ways as a severe constraint upon the present study.

The second limitation was the opposing pulls upon the researcher by the demands of a macro-level survey and a micro-level indepth analysis. To an extent, this was resolved in the present study. However, a good deal of the research effort has produced generalizations that lack the rigour of micro-level studies. Nonetheless, the macro-level observations made and conclusions reached have their own advantages, where none existed.

The third limitation arose, as has been pointed out in the Chapter on Methodology for the frequent communal riots that used to erupt while the field work was in progress. This often led to discontinuity in the interviews, as it was difficult to visit the informants and the respondents.

Fourth, there was the great reliance upon informants. Since, our effort was to reconstruct with their help, events that had occurred over thirty years ago there was no way of very strictly checking the reliability and validity of their accounts. However, two precautionary steps were taken. Firstly, reliance was not placed upon just a small group and, further, even the large number of informants contacted were not from any one socio-economic strata. By selecting informants from various strata, it was hoped that a more balanced view would emerge.

Finally, it may be admitted that a study like this has not been able to either depend upon or generate any theoretical formulations regarding the sociological understanding of social change, but to a certain extent Arnold Toynbee's theory of challenge and response was found relevant in the present context. The immediate response to the challenge of Police Action was negative in the upper and lower classes but positive in the middle class. Of course, the situation that was surveyed and studied was culturally as well as historically specific, and such situation and their studies do not easily lend themselves to any theorizing. Also, the circumstances of the study required it to be in the nature of an exploratory—descriptive study. The nature of the study could not be analytic. But if follow-up studies are undertaken some theoretical analysis be hopefully possible.

Suggestions for further studies: Turning now to the suggestions for further studies, it may first be pointed out that studies like the present one need to be repeated with greater rigour than was possible in the present study. This study can now serve as a sort of a bench-mark survey, which is indicative of the times along which other macro and micro studies can now be undertaken. At the macro level more systematic surveys of Hyderabadi Muslims need to be undertaken so that a more comprehensive picture of social change can emerge. Due to the constraints under which an individual researcher works, and that too for doctoral research, the present study could focus attention only upon selected areas of social life. More extensive surveys, as well as in-depth intensive investigations, can now follow to give us a more detailed account.

More specifically, we need further research on the changing status of women and the interactional dynamics of the family. In the present study, it had not been possible to study the interactional aspects. Similarly, we need to know more about Muslim youth and their problems of adjustment and response to contemporary changes that are occurring in the Indian society. Actually, these studies could also have a comparative dimension, in which it should be possible to compare and contract the adjustment and response patterns of Hyderabadi Muslims with that of North Indian Muslims, especially, say, in towns like Lucknow, and Aligarh on the one hand, and, Rampur, (which is an erstwhile, Muslim dominated state) on the other hand, to modernizing trends of the wider Indian society.

It is also suggested that studies of political mobilization of Hyderabadi Muslims, following economic affluence need to be conducted. In the course of our field work it had come to the knowledge of the researcher that the *mashaegeen* (reference to whom has been made in Chapter IV) and their influence have not vanished despite modernization. A more detailed study of this group should bring to light valuable data concerning the linkage between modernization and faith in such intermediaries.

Finally, the time has now also come for sociologists, and other social scientists, to take stock of the changes that are again creeping into the Muslim society of Hyderabad due to the gradual end of the Gulf boom. Newspapers and other media have already started bringing this fact and its repercussions, to our attention. However, these accounts are cursory and not analytical, and, hence, sociologists (and others) must do the needful. In case of Hyderabadi Muslims, such analyses are all the more necessary because in the decades following the major upheaval of 1948, this will be yet another important development in the lives of Hyderabadi Muslims. The Gulf boom has rescued them from a depressing situation, will they now gradually descend into another abyss of gloom and frustration, or have they developed, due to the experience of recent decades, a capability to adjust and respond to the challenges confronting them? Sociologists need not wait for time to answer these questions.

APPENDICES

APPENDIX I

Civil List of Hyderabad 1931

Posts	Muslims	Hindus	Others	Total
1. Secretaries	10	1	1	12
2. Additional Secretaries	2	1	1	4
3. Joint Secretaries	3	Nil	Nil	3
4. Deputy Secretaries	9	3	Nil	12
5. Assistant Secretaries	55	8	Nil	63
6. Heads of Depts	40	6	1	47
7. Subedars	4	Nil	Nil	4
8. Collectors	14	2	Nil	16
9. Revenue Board	2	Nil	Nil	2
10. Sub-Collectors	50	19	2	71
11. Tahsildars	75	40	4	119
12. High Court Judges	8	5	Nil	13
13. Magistrates and Munsifs	147	33	Nil	180
14. Police (DSP, ASP) and circle inspectors	73	12	6	91
15. Education Officers	237	65	27	329
16. Supply Officers	25	7	1	33
	754	202	43	999
	75	20	5	100

Gazetteer—Government of Hyderabad 1931.

APPENDIX II

(A letter of H.C.S. Officer)

Fareed Mirza,
House No. 15, Nizam Lines
Gosha Mahal, Hyderabad
Deccan
Dated : 13th May, 1949

To

Mr. Jatley
Inspector General of Police
Hyderabad State

Sir,

Twice I visited Tamsa, a big village in Hudgaon Tahsil in Nanded District after Police Action. I want to bring some facts to your kind notice.

First time, when the Indian Military visited this place, many Muslims were killed, all their houses were looted, some of them were burnt by goondas and some by the Military men. After a few days, on 14th October 1949, Union Sub-Inspector of Police with his constables came here and took charge of this Police Station House. The same day some Military officers also came. All the male Muslims were asked to assemble in front of Congress house. The Muslims complied with the command. Most of Muslims were beaten, kicked and insulted in many ways by some goondas in the presence of hundreds of non-Muslims and many Military and police officers.

The most regrettable and serious thing happened on 23rd October 1948. Some twenty-six young Muslims were dragged from their houses and kept under the custody of military men stationed at Tamsa. In the evening three Muslims were left, the remaining 23 were taken into jungle in the night, and shot dead. The shots were heard by many men in Tamsa. Many selected Hindus had gone to jungle to watch this performance of cold blooded murder of twenty-three young Muslims. It is rumoured that the military men were hesitating to do such a cruel thing, because it was a long time after the Military action had taken place there. But they were won over when the Saits, Sahukars and others collected ten thousand rupees and gave to them to perform such a horrible job. The man who played the main part in this murder of 23 able bodied Muslims was...Havaldar who was in charge of Indian Military men stationed there. Now he is working at Hadgaon proper in Nanded District.

Mr. Verma, Deputy Civil Administrator of Nanded District had recorded statements of some inhabitants of Tamsa about this and other happenings. Till now nothing has happened. I beg to suggest that a Maharathi knowing officer from your intelligence department may be sent there to ascertain facts. I can give the name of these 23 Muslims who were shot dead on 23rd October 1948 if you think it necessary.

Yours sincerely
Sd/- Fareed Mirza
Member, Central
Relief Committee

APPENDIX III

Table I

Showing Family Background and Mobility Pattern of the Respondents

		Upper Class					*Middle Class*					*Lower Class (Sk)*			*Lower Class (Unsk)*			
Background		*Civil Servant*	*Lawyer*	*Doctor*	*Engineer*	*U.T.*	*S.T.*	*Clerk*	*Typist*	*H.I.*	*D.H.E.*	*Driver*	*Tailor*	*Welder*	*Electrician*	*Rickshaw-puller*	*D.S.*	*Beggar*
Feudal aristocrats	20	7	2			1						2				5	2	1
Lawyers	8		6			2												
University teachers	2					2												
Tehsildars	4									3	1							
Clarks	45	2	1	8	7	2	4	6	4	3	4		1	2	1			
School teachers	26	1	1	2	3	3	3	4	4	2	3							

Police Inspectors	4						1		1		2							
Shopkeepers	2						1			1								
Army soldiers	3						1		1	1								
Drivers	5											5						
Tailors	5												5					
Welders	4													4				
Electrician	5														5			
Police Constables	5											1	1	2	1			
Beggars	15															2	4	9
Domestic servants	7															3	4	
	160	10	10	10	10	10	10	10	10	10	10	8	7	8	7	10	10	10

U.T.=University teacher; S.T.=School teacher; H.I.=Health inspector; D.H.E.=Diploma holder Engineer; D.S.=Domestic Servant

Table II

Showing Family Background of the Respondents' Wives

Family Background of the Family	*Upper Class*					*Middle Class*					*Lower Class (Sk)*				*Lower Class (Unsk)*		
	Civil servant	*Lawyer*	*Doctor*	*Engineer*	*U.T.*	*S.T.*	*Clerk*	*Typist*	*H.I.*	*D.H.E.*	*Driver*	*Tailor*	*Welder*	*Electrician*	*Domestic servant*	*Rickshaw puller*	*Beggar*
Civil servant	3	2			2												
Lawyers	2	3			3												
Army officers	2	2			2												
Jagirdars	2	1			1												
Tehsildars			1 (H)	2		1	2	1	1	3							
Police commissioner	1	2		2													
Clerks			4	3	1	2	4	3	3	1							

Police inspectors			1	2		1	2	2	2	4							
School teachers			2		1	5	1	2	2								
Soldiers				1		1	1	2	2	2							
Drivers											4		1		3		
Tailors												4	1				
Carpenter											1		1	3	2		
Domestic servants			2 (Ch)								3		1	2	5	4	
Police constables												3	2			2	
Shopkeepers			•										2	2		2	
Beggars																2	10
	10	10	10	10	10	10	10	10	10	10	8	7	8	7	10	10	10

U.T.=University teacher; S.T.=School teacher; H.I.=Health inspector; D.H.E.=Diploma holder Engineer

Table III

Showing the level of Education of the Respondents' Wives

Education of Respondents' Wives	*U.C.*					*M.C.*					*L.C. (Skilled)*				*L.C. (Unskilled)*			
	Civil servant	*Lawyers*	*Doctor*	*Engineer*	*U.T.*	*S.T.*	*Clerk*	*Typist*	*H.I.*	*D.H.E.*	*Driver*	*Tailor*	*Welder*	*Electrician*	*D.S.*	*Rickshaw puller*	*Beggar*	*Total*
Illiterate											6	4	5	1	4	8	10	38
Can read Quran											2	2	2	4	2	1		13
Can read and write Urdu								1				1	1	2	4	1		10
Educated upto V std							1		1									2
Educated upto VIII						2		4	4	2								12
Non-matric						1	2	1	3	3								10
Matric						2		1										3
Basic trained						3	2	1	2	1								9

Intermediate	6	6	2	9	4		2	1										30
Graduate	2	4	2	1		1	2			1								13
B. Ed.	2				3	1	1	1		2								10
M.B.B.S.			6															6
B.E.																		—
LL.B.																		—
Postgraduate					3					1								4
Ph.D.																		—
	10	10	10	10	10	10	10	10	10	10	8	7	8	7	10	10	10	160

U.T.=University teacher; S.T.=School teacher; H.I.=Health inspector; D.H.E.=Diploma holder engineer; D.S.=Domestic Servant; U C.=Upper Class; M.C.=Middle Class; L.C.=Lower Class

Table IV

Education of the Children of the Respondents

Education of Children	*Civil servant*		*Lawyer*		*Doctor*		*Engi-neer*		*U.T.*		*S.T.*		*Clerk*		*Typist*		*H.I.*		*D.H.E.*	
	M	*F*	*M*	*F*	*M*	*F*	*M*	*F*	*M*	*F*	*M*	*F*	*M*	*F*	*M*	*F*	*M*	*F*	*M*	*F*
1	*2*	*3*	*4*	*5*	*6*	*7*	*8*	*9*	*10*	*11*	*12*	*13*	*14*	*15*	*16*	*17*	*18*	*19*	*20*	*21*
Illiterate																				
Can read Quran																				
Can read & write Urdu																				
Educated upto V std																				
Educated upto VIII																				
Non-matric																				
Matric																				
Basic trained																				
Intermediates												4		4				1		1
Graduates											6	10	3	4	12		7	11	7	10

B.Ed.						2					4	7	2	6	2	4		2		2
M.B.B.S.	8	11	11	6	11	8	10	6	7	6	2	3	2	4	5	3	8	7	12	9
B.E.	9	2	7		6		8	2	8		2		2		2		6		8	
LL.B.			4	2																
Postgraduates	5	5	2	6	1	3	4	6	4	10	3	4	3	3	2	2		2		3
Ph.D.									2											
Total	22	18	24	14	18	13	22	14	21	16	17	29	12	21	23	11	21	23	27	25
	40		38		31		36		37		45		33		34		44		52	

(*Contd.*)

TABLE IV (*Contd.*)

Education of Children	*Driver*		*Tailor*		*Weldsr*		*E.*		*D.S.*		*R.P.*		*Beggar*	
	M	*F*	*M*	*F*	*M*	*F*	*M*	*F*	*M*	*F*	*M*	*F*	*M*	*F*
	22	*23*	*24*	*25*	*26*	*27*	*28*	*29*	*30*	*31*	*32*	*33*	*34*	*35*
Illiterate	10	5	9	5	5	4	5	2	15	13	20	20	24	32
Can read Quran									8	7	4	4	2	3
Can read & write Urdu	7	9	8	5	12	4	4	4	6	4	1	2		
Education upto V std	3	4	6	4	3	3	8	4	7	2	3			
Education upto VIII	2	3	1	3	1	2		2						
Non-matric	4	1	2	1	2	2	2	1						
Matric	1		1		1	1			2	1	1	1		
Basic trained				1	1	1		2						
Intermediates						1	1	1						
Graduates														
B.Ed.														
M.B.B.S.														

B.E.														
LL.B.														
Postgraduates														
Ph.D.														
Total	27	22	27	19	25	18	20	16	38	27	29	27	26	35
	49		46		43		36		65		56		61	

U.T. = University Teachers; S.T. = School Teachers; H.I. = Health Inspectors;
D.H.E. = Diploma Holder Engineers; E. = Electricians; D.S. = Domestic Servants;
R.P. = Rickshaw Pullers.

Upper Glass		Middle Class		Lower Class (Skilled)		Lower Class (Unskilled)	
Male	= 107	Male	= 100	Male	= 99	Male	= 99
Female	= 75	Female	= 108	Female	= 75	Female	= 89
Total	= 182	Total	= 208	Total	= 174	Total	= 182

Total Children = 746
Total Male = 393
Total Female = 347

Table V

Showing Profession of the Wives of the Respondents

	Upper Class				*Middle Class*						*Lower Class (Skilled)*				*Lower Class (Unskilled)*		
Profession of the wives	*Civil servant*	*Lawyer*	*Doctor*	*Engineer*	*U.T.*	*S.T.*	*Clerk*	*Typist*	*H.I.*	*D.H.E.*	*Driver*	*Tailor*	*welder*	*Electrician*	*Domestic servant*	*R.K.*	*Beggar*
Housewives	8	10	2	8	4	4	3	5	5	3		3	6	6		3	
Inspectoress of school	2																
Doctors			6														
University teachers					3												
School teachers			2	2	3	4	3	2	2	3							
Clerks							2	1	1	2							
Typists						2	2	2	2								
Bank employee										1							

Ayas in schools and colleges											4	3	1			
Beggars																
Fruit & vegetable vendors															3	2
Domestic servants											4	1	1	1	7	5
	10	10	10	10	10	10	10	10	10	10	8	7	8	7	10	10

U.T. = University teacher; S.T. = School teacher; H.I. = Health Inspector;
D.H.E. = Dip. holder Engineer

Housewives	= 32	Housewives	= 20	Housewives	= 15	Housewives	= 3
School teachers	= 27	Clerks	= 9	Ayas	= 8	Beggars	= 10
Inspectoress of school	= 2	Typist	= 8	Domestic servants	= 7	Fruit and vegetable vendors	= 5
University teachers	= 3	School teachers	= 14			Domestic servants	= 12
Doctors	= 6	Bank employee	= 1				
		University teachers	= 1				

Table VI

Showing Profession of the Respondents' Male Children

Profession of the respondents' male children	*Upper Class*					*Middle Class*					*Lower Class (Sk)*				*Lower Class (Unsk)*		
	Civil Servant	*Lawyer*	*Doctor*	*Engineer*	*U.T.*	*S.T.*	*Clerk*	*Typist*	*H.I.*	*D.H.E.*	*Driver*	*Tailor*	*Welder*	*Electrician*	*Domestic servant*	*Rickshaw puller*	*Beggar*
Unemployed						4	2	3	5	6					6	8	
Beggars																1	7
Factory workers															11	6	10
Police constable															1		
Shopkeepers											2	1	1	1	2	2	
Postmen											1				4	1	
Vegetable and fruit vendors															2	2	6
Motor mechanic															1	4	
Peon											1			1	5	3	

Domestic servants																	5
Typists						2	1	4	1	1	2						
Clerks						3	1	7	1					2			
Drivers											15	5	2	2	4	2	
Tailors											2	19	2	2			
Welders											3	1	19	1			
Electricians											1	1	1	11			
School teachers						2	1	2		2					2		
Doctors	8	11	11	10	7	2	3	3	8	10							
Engineers	9	7	6	8	8	1	2	2	6	8							
University teachers				1	2	3	2	2									
Civil servants	5	2	1														
Lawyers		4															
Bank employees				1	2												
Research scholars				2	2												
Total	22	24	18	22	21	17	12	23	21	27	27	27	25	20	38	29	26

U.T.=University teachers; S.T.=School teachers; H.I.=Health Inspectors; D.H E.=Diploma holder Engineer.

Table VII

Profession of Female Children of the Respondents

Profession of the Female Children	*U.C.*					*M.C.*					*L.C. (Skilled)*				*L.C. (Unskilled)*		
	Civil servant	*Lawyer*	*Doctor*	*Engineer*	*U.T.*	*S.T.*	*Clerk*	*Typist*	*H.I.*	*D.H.E.*	*Driver*	*Tailor*	*Welder*	*Electrician*	*Domestic servant*	*Rickshaw puller*	*Beggar*
Unemployed	2	3	2	3	3	8	6	3	6	8		6	3	3			
Housewives						1	3	1	4	6	3	5	6	6	4	8	
Beggars																	20
Factory workers															8	10	5
Vegetable and fruit vendors															1		
Domestic servants											9	3	3		8	4	10

Ayas in school and colleges											6	4	5	3	6	5	
Typists						3	2	2	1	2	1			2			
Clerks						2	2	2	2	2							
School teachers	2		2	1	3	8	3		2	2	3	1	1	2			
Doctors	11	6	8	6	5	3	4	3	7	3							
Engineers				2													
University teachers	3	2	1	2	4	1	1		1	2							
Bank employees		2				2											
Research scholars					1												
Lawyers		1															
Total	18	14	13	14	16	28	21	11	23	25	22	19	18	16	27	27	35

U.T.=University teacher; S.T.=School teacher; H.I.=Health inspector; D.H.E.=Dip. holder engineer.

U.C.=Upper Class; M.C.=Middle Class; L.C. (Sk)=Lower Class (Skilled); L.C. (Unsk)=Lower Class (Unskilled).

Glossary

Aap—You.

Aashoorkhana—Place where Alums are installed.

Aflas—Misery.

Ahlekar—Clerk.

Ajlaf—Downtrodden.

Alum—Stick covered with cloth and a metal palm tied on top as a symbol of head. It is a symbol of memory of martyrs in Karbala with Imam Hussain.

Amal—Master of witchcraft.

Amir—Rich, noble.

Anna—Maid servant employed for breast feeding to babies.

Aqiqa—Muslim ceremony when a baby's head was clean shaven for the first time.

Aukaf—Endowment.

Ausat tabqa—Middle class.

Aya—Maid servant to look after children—also female peon.

Azad pesha—Independent professional.

Azan—Call for prayers.

Baghare Baigan—Special dish of stuffed brinjals.

Bagloos—Ornamental belt.

Bala—Evil spirit.

Barra Katha—Hindu religious gathering (in South).

Bhajanmandali—Hindu religious gathering.

Bismillah- Caremony when the child is four years four months and four days old. He is made to read for first time out of Holy Quran.

Chauthi—Dinner hosted by the brides party after marriage.

Chehlum—A ceremony performed on the fortieth day after death.

Chakna—A dish prepared with intestines of sheep.

Chokri—A girl servant.

Chudidar pajama—Tight trousers.

Damki Murghi—Roasted chicken.

Darbar—A royal court.

Dargah—Moslum of saints.

Dastar—Distinctive turbans worn by Nizam's officials.

Deori—Palace.

Dupattah—A cloth thrown loosely over the head and shoulder by women.

Ekka—A horse driven carriage.

Farman—Royal order—decree.

Fatiha—Prayers for the dead.

Gharara—Dress worn by women in U.P.

Ghurba—Poor.

Haft—Seven.

Haj—Muslim pilgrimage.

Hakeem—Physician, doctor of eastern medicine (unani).

Harem—Women's section of an appartment—also used for keeps.

Hari katha—Religious gathering of Hindu (in South).

Idi—Tip given on the occasion of Id.

Idgah—An open space on the outskrits of the city where special prayers were held.

Iftar—Snacks taken at the time of breaking the fast.

Itar—Perfume.

Jagir—A plot of land allotted to someone as a reward or to maintain troops.

Jagirdar—Holder of jagir and recipient of its revenue.

Jatara—A pilgrimage to a place of sanctity performed by Hindus, when the deity of the temple is taken out in huge wooden carriage with pomp and pageantry.

Jazia tax—Tax imposed by Muslim rulers on non-Muslim subjebts.

Jode-ki-Raqam—Cash given at the time of marriage to the groom by bride's party.

Jumagi—A part of marriage of ceremonies. Celebrated on every Friday after marriage for five weeks.

Khatta—Dish of tamarind juice.

Khirat—Alms.

Kaymkhani—Rajput converts to Islam.

Khawas—Permanent keep.

Kheer—A dish with rice cooked in milk and pulverised.

Khichdi—Dish made of split pulse and rice.

Khada Duppata—A piece of cloth 5 metres in length worn by Muslim women in Deccan.

Khitab—Title given by the king.

Kismat—Fate.

Koonda—An earthen ware vessel in which eatables are kept.

Paigah—Noble families of honour which had marital relations with the royal family.

Palakda—An adopted child of low birth.

Pan—betels.

Pandan—A beautiful box for keeping betel leaves and items needed for.

Papad—Wafers of pulse mixed with spices.

Peshkar—Administrative officer.

Patel—A headman of village. Collects revenue and maintain law and order.

Patwari—A village accountant.

Punja—A metal palm to symbolise head on the Alum.

Purdah—An institution of segregation of women.

Qassab—Butcher.

Qawal—Professional singers of qawali (songs sung in a typical style).

Samastan—Hindu noble or chief family, area ruled by such a family. (It is an equal of jagirdar).

Sanchak—Ceremony at bride's place just one day before marriage.

Labbe—Muslims leather merchants from Madras.

Ladaf—Muslim cotton merchants in Hyderabad.

Majlis—Meetings to mourn the killing of Imam Hussain at Karbala.

Marsia—Elegy in memory of Imam Hussain.

Manja—A ceremony before the nikah which marks the beginning of marriage.

Mankooha—A legal wife other than the wife of marriage.

Mehndi—A ceremony at the groom's place just one day before marriage.

Mujavar—Persons responsible for maintaining the ashoor-khanan.

Mulazim sarkar—Government servant.

Najeeb-ut-Tarfain—Progeny of a Saiyid mother and father.

Nauha—Elegy in the memory of Imam Hussain.

Nazar—A present of offering, specially from an inferior to superior.

Niaz—Offering by way of dedication through prayers on special occasions such as the birthday of the Holy Prophet and on anniversaries of saints, delicious dishes were prepared and fatiha recited. The food is distributed among poor or friends and relatives are entertained.

Sendi—Toddy—A local intoxicant from the palm tree.

Shakram—A carriage driven by two bullocks covered from all sides.

Sharbat—Cold drink.

Suba—Province.

Subedar—Incharge of a suba.

Taraveeh—Special namaz offered at night in the month of Ramzan.

Tazia—Replica of shrine of Hassan and Hussain associated with Muharram.

Taveez—Small piece of paper with certain inscriptions on it. Used as an instrument of witchcraft.

Teli Raja—Special beggar that came in the month of Tertezi.

Toreposh—Beautiful cloth used to cover 'khans' or huge trays containing eatables.

Umra—Nobles.

Umara-e-uzzam—Nobles of the highest order.

Urs—Anniversary of a saint.

Waaz—A religious speech.

Waguzasht—Lifting of confiscation.

Walima—Dinner given by the groom's party after marriage.

Wazu—Washing of face, hands and feet before offering namaz.

Zabti—Confiscation.

Zamindar—Landlord.

Zanana—Women's quarters.

Bibliography

Ahmed, Aziz, "Aisee Balandi Aisse Pasti" (Urdu) Modern Publishing House, 1986 (latast edition).

Ahmed, Imtiaz (ed.), "Family Kinship and Marriage among Muslims in India". Manohar Book Service, 1976.

Ahmed, Imtiaz (ed)., "Rituals and Religion among Muslims in India". Manohar Publications, 1981.

Ahmed, Imtiaz (ed.), "Modernization and Social Change Muslims in India", Manohar Publications, 1983.

Ahmed, Imtiaz (ed.), "Caste and Social Stratification among the Muslims", Manohar Book Service. 1983.

Ahmed, Zahir, "Life's Yesterday". Thacker and Co., Ltd., Bombay 1945.

Alam, Shah Manzoor, "Hyderabad—Secundrabad: A Study in Urban Geography", Allied Publishers, 1965.

Ali, Fida, "Tarikh-e-Farishta (Urdu translation), Osmania University Press, 1926.

Ali, Hasham Amir, "Facts and Fancies", The Dominion Book Concern, 1947.

Ali, Mir Laiq, "Tragedy of Hyderabad", Pakistan Cooperative Book Society, Karachi, 1962.

Ansari, Ghaus, "Muslim Caste in Utter Pradesh" Ethnographic and Cultural Society, U.P., Lucknow, India, 1960.

Ashraf, K.M., "Life and Conditions of the People of Hindustan", Delhi, 1959.

Banu, Jilani, "Aiwane-i-Gazal" (Urdu Novel), Novelistan, New Delhi, 1976.

Betteille, A., "Caste, Class and Power Changing Social Stratification in a Tanjore Village", Berkely, 1966.

Betteille, A. (ed.), "Social Inequality". Penguin Books Ltd., England.

Bilgrami, Hosh, "Mushahedat" (Obsersations) (Urdu) Inqlab Press, Hyderabad, 1950.

Campbell, C.A., "Glimpses of the Nizam's Dominion", C.B. Burrows, 1898.

Champakalakshmi, N., "The Economic and Social Life of the Peasantry in the Deccan in the 19th Century", Intikab Press.

Daryabadi, A.M., "Tasaurat-e-Deccan" (Urdu), Bhadur Yar Jung Acadmy, 1977.

Gauba, K.L., "Passive Voices—A Penetrating Study of Muslims in India", Thacker & Co. Ltd., Bombay, 1973.

Gauba, K.L., "Hyderabad or India", Raj Kamal Publications, Delhi, 1948.

Harman, S., "Plight of Muslims in India", D.L. Publication, London, 1976.

Hashmi, N., "Hyderabad-Ki-Niswani Duniya" (Urdu), Idare Adabe Jadeed, Hyderabad, 1944.

Hashmi, N., "Deccani Culture", Aliya Printers, Lahore, 1923 (Urdu).

Hassan, A.Z.M., "Tazkera Mashret-e-Hyderabad Deccan" (Urdu), Talegu Urdu Acadmy, Hyderabad, 1967.

Hassan, Z., "Deccan Udas Hai Yaro" (Urdu), Hussaini Book Depot, Hyderabad, 1978.

Huda, M.W., "Inside Hyderabad", Urdu Markaz, Karachi, 1947.

Hussain, A., "Destiny of Indian Muslim", Asia Publishing House, 1965.

Hussain, S.A., "Whither Hyderabad? A Brief Study of Some of the Outstanding Problems of the Premier Indian States", Published by the author, Hyderabad, 1935.

Jaferi, Rais Ahmed, "Hyderabad Jo Kabhi Tha", Kitab Manzil, Lahore, 1960.

Jain, S., "Modernization of Muslims of Jaipur", Rawat Publication, Jaipur, 1986.

Jeffery, P., "Frogs in the Well", Vikas Publication, Delhi, 1979.

Jung, A.Y., "Hyderabad in Retrospect", Times of India Publication, Bombay, 1949.

Khan, K.G.H., "Gulzar-e-Asafia" (Urdu), United India Press, Hyderabad, 1287 Hijri.

Khan, M.F., "A History of the Administrative Reforms in Hyderabad State", New Hyderabad Press, 1935.

Karaka, D.F., "Fabulous Mughal, Nizam VII of Hyderabad", Jerek Verschoyle, London, 1958.

Levy, R., "The Social Structure of Islam, Second Edition of the Sociology of Islam", Cambridge University Press, 1957.

Lynten, H.R. & Mohini, R., "The Days of the Beloved", London University of California Press, 1974.

Malihabadi, Josh, "Yadon-Ki-Barat", Lucknow Aa-i-ne Adab (Urdu), 1972.

Manzoor-ul Amin, Rafia, "Alam Panah" (Urdu Novel), Novelistan, Delhi, 1982.

Menon, I., "Status of Muslim Women in India—A Case Study of Kerala", Uppal Publishing House, New Delhi, 1981.

Menon, V.P., "The History of Integration of Indian States", Bhartiya Vidya Bhavan, 1960.

Mirza, Fareed, "Pre and Post Police Action Days in Erstwhile Hyderabad State: What I Sw, Felt and Did", Published by the author, 1976.

Mudiraj, K.K., "Pictorial Hyderabad", Chandrakanta Press, Hyderabad, 1934.

Mujeeb, M., "The Indian Muslims", George Allen & Unwin, London, 1967.

Munshi, K.M., "The End of an Era", Bharatiya Vidya Bhavan, Bombay.

Naidu, Ratna, "Inner City of Hyderabad", study sponsored by Government of India 1980.

Prasad, D., "Fair and Festival", Dept. of Tourism, Govt. of A.P., 1982.

Prasad, R., "The Asif Jahis of Hyderabad", Vikas Publishing House, Pvt. Ltd., 1984.

Regani, S., "Nizam British Relations 1724-1857", Swaraja Printing Works. Secundrabad, 1963.

Raj, Sheela, "Mediavalism to Modernism—Socio-economic and Cultural History of Hyderabad 1869-1911", Popular Prakashan Ltd., Bombay, 1987.

Sarkar, Jadunath, "History of Deccan", Vol. II, Sarkar & Sons, 1930.

Shakaib, Badar, "Hyderabad-Ka-Urooj-O-Zawal" (Urdu), Karachi, 1964.

Sherwani, Haroon Khan, Shariq-e-Deccan" (Urdu), Shamsul Maktaba, Hyderabad, 1942.

Sherwani, H.K., "Deccan Culture", Anjuman Islam Urdu Research Institute, Hyderabad.

Sibgathullah, M., "Gulgashat-e-Deccan (Urdu), Nami Press, Lucknow, 1932.

Siddiqui, A.M., "Tareeq Golcunda" (Urdu), Maktab-e-Ibrahimia, Hyderabad, 1939.

Siddiqui, M.K., "Muslims of Calcutta—A Study in Aspects of their Social Organization", Anthropological Survey of India, Govt. of India, 1974.

Smith, W.C., "Modern Islam in India—A Social Analysis", Ripon Printing Press, 1947.

Sunder, Sham B., "Riyasat-e-Hyderabad Aur Past Aquam" (Urdu), Intezami Press, Hyderabad, 1944.

Tirth, Swami Ramanand, "Momairs of Hyderabad—Freedom Struggle", Popular Publication, Bombay, 1967.

Tourche, Theo W. Dela, "Twenty five years as Ruler of Hyderabad", Excelsior Press, Secundrabad, 1936.

Vreede-de-Steurs, Cora, "Pardah: A Study of North Indian Muslim Women", New York, 1969.

Zore, Mohiuddin Qadri, "Farkhunda Buniyad Hyderabad" (Urdu), Hyderabad, Sabras Kitabgarh, 1952.

Zore, M.Q., "Sultan Mohammed Quli Qutub Shah" (Urdu), Azam Steam Press, 1940.

Reports and Articles in Journals

The Central Records Office, Hyderabad Government, Hyderabad Central Office, Chronology of Modern Hyderabad, 1720-1890, 1954.

Hassan, Syed Majeedul, "Employment of Hyderabadi Muslims in Gulf Countries", Institute of Muslim Minority Affairs, King Abdul Aziz University, Jeddah, 1982.

Hyderabad Finance Department, Economic Adviser, "Review of Hyderabad Finance", 1961.

The Indian Institute of Economics, "A Socio-Economic Survey of Rickshaw-Drivers in Hyderabad", Hyderabad, 1962.

The Indian Institute of Economics, "Report on a Socio-Economic and Health Survey of Street-Beggars in Hyderabad—Secunderabad City Area", 1956.

The Indian Institute of Economics, "A Socio-Economic Survey of Hut-Dwellers in Hyderabad City", Hyderabad, 1959.

Khan, Wahiduddin (Dr.) Director, Centre for Economic and Social Studies, Hyderabad, "Economic Survey of SETWIN", Hyderabad, 1983.

Khusro, A.M., "Economic and Social Effects of Jagirdari Abolition and Land Reform in Hyderabad", Osmania University Press, 1958.

Ramesan, N. (ed.), "The Freedom Struggle in Hyderabad", (four volumes) A.P. Committee for the Compilation of a History of Freedom Struggle in Andhra Pradesh, Hyderabad, 1966.

Smith, W.C., "Hyderabad a Muslim Tragedy", Middle East Journal, Vol. 4, No. 1, Canada McGrill University, Jan. 1950.

Goud, Raj Bahadur (ed.), "Glorious Telangana Armed Struggle", Communist Party Publication, No. 8, March 1983.

The Syaset (Urdu Daily), "Khadim Sher Ka Maashi Survey" (Urdu) (Economic Survey of the old city), Hyderabad, 1984.

Ahmed, Imtiaz, "The Ashraf-Ajlaf Dichotomy in Muslims Social Structure in India", Indian Economic and Social History Review, 3(3), pp. 268-278, 1966.

Hyderi, Sir M. Akbar, "Hyderabad Today", Journal of the East India Association, 22 London, January 1931.

Khan, Rashiduddin, "A Society in Change", Seminar No. 100, April 1967.

Khan, Rashiduddin, "Muslim Leadership and Electoral Politics in Hyderabad—A Pattern of Minority Articulation", Economic and Political Weekly, Vol. VI, Nos. 15 and 16, April 10 and 17, 1971.

Khundmiri, S.A., "Alienation of Muslims—Need for a Commonsense Approachi", Secular Democracy Annual Number 1969.

Moazzam, Anwar, "The Dilemma of Dual Personality", Secular Democracy, Vol. 3, No. 9, Sept. 1970.

Mohiuddin, Makhdum, "Urdu Literature in Andhra Pradesh", p. 23, Illustrated Weekly of India, Sept. 11, 1966.

Newspapers

Deccan Chronicle, Hyderabad.

The Hindu, Madras.

Imroz (Urdu Daily), Hyderabad.

Payam (Urdu Daily), Hyderabad.

Rahber-e-Deccan (Urdu Daily), Hyderabad.

Rahnuma-e-Deccan (Urdu Daily), Hyderabad.

The Times of India, Bombay.

Syaset (Urdu Daily), Hyderabad.

Dissertations

Ali, Hasham Amir, "Westernization of Hyderabad State", Cornel University, Ph.D. Dissertation, 1929.

Ali, Talat, "Impact of Westernization on the Muslim Community of Hyderabad", Ph.D. Dissertation, Osmania University, 1983.

Hussaini, Syed Khalilullah, "Social and Cultural Demands of Deccan Muslims", M.A. Dissertation, Osmania University, 1948.

Imadi, Mohd. Abdul Khadir, "Nobles of Hyderabad—A Study in Social Change", Ph.D. Dissertation in Sociology, Osmania University, 1977.

Khan, Masood Ali, "Social Change Among the Muslims of Aurangabad", Ph.D. Dissertation in Sociology, Marathwad University, 1977.

Khan, Munir Ahmed, "Muslim Politics in Hyderabad", Ph.D. Dissertation in Political Science, Osmania University, 1980.

Omer, Sultan, "Public Policy towards Muslims—A Case Study of Hyderabad", M.Phil. Dissertation, Osmania University, 1980.

Prasad, Dharmindra, "Social and Cultural Geography of Hyderabad City—A Historical Perspective", Ph.D. Dissertation, Osmania University, 1982.

Zubaida, Asma, "Social Stratification among the Muslims of Hyderabad", M.Phil. Dissertation in Sociology, Osmania University, 1980.

Index